Toward Understanding
the Bible

By
GEORGIA HARKNESS

ABINGDON PRESS
New York • *Nashville*

TOWARD UNDERSTANDING THE BIBLE

Copyright MCMLII and MCMLIV by Georgia Harkness

PRINTED IN THE UNITED STATES OF AMERICA

Preface

The purpose of this book is to try to help the ordinary person get a better understanding of the Bible. That there is still a live interest in the Bible is evidenced by the fact that over two and one half million copies of the Revised Standard Version have been sold. That many people find spiritual refreshment from reading selected parts of it is certain. But that people in general, either within or outside of the churches, find the Bible as a whole to be meaningful is open to serious question. The greatest of all books is a closed book to many who do not understand its historical backgrounds, its diversity of literary form, or the unity in diversity of its spiritual message.

The Bible was written in a historical setting and culture very different from our own. It was written by men who had something from God to say to their times but who had no idea that they were writing Scripture to be read two or three thousand years later. Yet they were men of deep spiritual insight, and through their words God still speaks to us with a timeless message. If this message is to be most fruitfully grasped, whether for cultural enrichment or the deepening of personal faith, we need to understand the Bible's structure and content.

This little book is not designed to answer all the complex questions of biblical interpretation. It is simply a preparatory statement by which to go to the Bible and see what it says, and its usefulness will largely be determined by the extent to which the reader goes beyond it to the Bible itself. There is little here that is not the common possession of present-day biblical scholarship, but I have tried to condense, simplify and arrange in easily usable form what the big books tell at greater length.

The book begins, accordingly, with a look at the place of the Bible in our culture, then an examination of the crucial question of what is meant by its being the inspired Word of God. The second chapter deals with the geographical, social and religious setting within which the Bible emerged. The next two canvass the stages of development and the literary types in the Old and New Testaments, with a brief look at the main theme of most of the books. The final chapter attempts to show how the great notes in the Christian faith regarding God, man and Jesus Christ are firmly imbedded in the Bible.

What is presented here is drawn from so many sources that there is no use of trying to acknowledge them. The bibliography will indicate what I regard as the most useful sources for further study. A special word of thanks is due to Miss Juanita Brown of the Woman's Division of Christian Service of The Methodist Church, whose request prompted the writing of the book, and to my colleague Dr. John Herbert Otwell for his careful reading and valuable suggestions.

Quotations from the American Standard Version of the Revised Bible, copyrighted 1929, and the Revised Standard Version of the Bible, copyrighted 1946 and 1952, are used by permission of the Division of Christian Education of the National Council of the Churches of Christ in the U. S. A. References to these versions are indicated in the footnotes by the initials A. S. V. and R. S. V. I have used these and also the King James Version, selecting in each instance the diction which seemed to me best to fit the point under discussion.

GEORGIA HARKNESS

Contents

CHAPTER ONE

The Bible as the Word of God

Why Read the Bible?

To some readers of this little manual on Bible study the question, "Why read the Bible?" may seem wholly superfluous. Of course one ought to read the Bible because it is the word of God and a nourisher of the Christian life! For others, to whom the Bible may be a time-honored but nevertheless largely mysterious book, the question has more significance. Let us begin then by looking at some reasons why the Bible, in spite of the mass of printed matter that comes pouring from the presses, is still the most important book in existence and why reading it is one of the most important things that any person today can do.

THE BIBLE IN OUR CULTURE

In the first place, the whole of our Western culture is saturated with the Bible. It appears in the most commonplace matters of daily speech. When some calamity is narrowly averted, I escape "with the skin of my teeth."[1] When a person loves somebody or something very much, he or she or it

---

[1] Job 19:20

is "the apple of his eye."[2] When one man admires another, the second is "a man after his own heart."[3] We take the morning paper and try to read in the events of the day "the signs of the times."[4] We press an electric button in our homes and have heat or light "in the twinkling of an eye."[5] Much that we do in our homes and in our churches and communities is "a labor of love."[6] Nevertheless, sometimes we work for "filthy lucre."[7]

There are persons all around us who are "the salt of the earth."[8] There are others whose main philosophy of life appears to be "to eat, and to drink, and to be merry."[9] Occasionally there are those we are tempted to call "whited sepulchres."[10] In many of life's decisions we are "at the parting of the way."[11] In such crises people are sometimes "at their wit's end,"[12] so they would like to "take the wings of the morning"[13] and escape from it all.

In the crisis among the nations the deepest desire of mankind is "on earth peace, good will toward men."[14] We long for the day when "men shall beat their swords into ploughshares and their spears into pruninghooks,"[15] and with economic security and contentment, every man may be able to "sit under his vine and under his fig tree."[16]

Even in the writing of a book one cannot escape these ever-present biblical injunctions. For if the person who writes is to have readers he must make what he says so clear that "he may run who reads it." [17] And as books are still written and

---

[2] Deut. 32:10
[3] I Sam. 13:14
[4] Matt. 16:3
[5] I Cor. 15:52
[6] I Thess. 1:3, R.S.V.

[7] I Tim. 3:2
[8] Matt. 5:13
[9] Eccles. 8:15
[10] Matt. 23:27
[11] Ezek. 21:21

[12] Ps. 107:27
[13] Ps. 139:9
[14] Luke 2:14
[15] Isa. 2:4
[16] Mic. 4:4
[17] Hab. 2:2

published on what seems an endless number of subjects, the reader is reminded that "of making of many books there is no end."[18]

But it is not alone in our daily speech that the influence of the Bible is reflected; the greatest of our art, music, and literature is filled with it. One cannot walk through any of the famous art galleries of Europe without finding "an endless line of splendor" in biblical themes. Too many Americans fail to appreciate such art because they do not have a background of biblical knowledge to understand what is being portrayed. Again, the music of the ages which sings its way into our souls, whether it be Handel's *Messiah,* Mendelssohn's *Elijah,* a Gregorian chant, or a Negro spiritual, is saturated with the words and the message of the Bible. Not all the great books have had a biblical basis, but many of them have. Without the Bible we should not have Dante and Chaucer, Milton's *Paradise Lost* and *Samson Agonistes,* Browning's *Saul,* or the deep spiritual notes that appear in the works of such writers as William Blake, Tennyson, Matthew Arnold, Emerson, and Whittier. Shakespeare makes many allusions to the Bible. The addresses of Abraham Lincoln, who as a boy had the Bible as one of the few books accessible to him, are filled with its great overtones.

In the twentieth century, though we are more biblically illiterate than in any previous day, the Bible still makes its impact upon our literature. Its influence appears in best sellers that deal specifically with biblical themes such as Thomas Mann's *Joseph and His Brothers;* Sholem Asch's *The Naza-*

---

[18] Eccles. 12:12

rene, The Apostle, and *Mary;* Lloyd Douglas' *The Robe* and *The Big Fisherman;* Dorothy Clarke Wilson's *Prince of Egypt* and *The Herdsman.* Fulton Oursler's *The Greatest Story Ever Told* has brought a fresh awareness of the Bible to many readers of daily newspapers. Less directly Bible centered, but with biblical titles and themes with which the Bible is concerned, are such books as Aldous Huxley's *Eyeless in Gaza,* John Steinbeck's *The Grapes of Wrath,* and Lillian Hellman's *The Little Foxes.* In spite of an appalling ignorance of the Bible in our time, it continues to be the world's best seller. Well over a million copies of the complete Bible, and millions of portions of it in more than one thousand languages and dialects into which it has been translated, are printed every year.

The extent to which the Bible is imbedded in our artistic and literary heritage would, even if no other factor were present, make a knowledge of the Bible imperative and highlight the cultural loss resulting from its exclusion from the public schools. It is indeed unfortunate that many students who are expected to get some knowledge of the *Iliad,* the *Odyssey,* the *Aeneid,* and of Shakespeare's plays have no acquaintance with a classic far greater and more influential than any of these. But beyond its literary significance there is still another element, of greater importance. This is the effect that it has had upon the moral and spiritual ideas of the Western world.

The most priceless political heritage of the Western world, for which both blood and treasure have been poured out so lavishly, is democracy. Democracy has its roots in the concept of the worth of every individual before God. This in turn mainly takes its rise from the New Testament. To go back no further than to the events that led to the founding of the American Republic, it was the Bible which nourished the Puritan revolt in England in the seventeenth century. It was the Bible and its message which brought large numbers of our founding fathers to this country and led them to establish an educational system "to foil the wiles of Satan" almost as soon as they had set foot upon American soil. It was the Bible which undergirded them to endure the hardships of the early days and to press westward to open up the frontier. It was the Bible which led to the establishment of free public schools and, through the Church, to a large number of church-related colleges. It has continued through the years to undergird not only sound learning but also sound morality. While obviously not all our political leaders have been churchmen or students of the Bible, its words and its spirit breathe through the great political utterances of our heritage from Washington and Jefferson through Daniel Webster and Abraham Lincoln and to the "four freedoms" of Franklin D. Roosevelt. One can scarcely be a good patriot, to say nothing of a good Christian, without acquaintance with this fountainhead of so much that is good in American life.

THE BIBLE AS LITERATURE

Not only is the Bible ingrained in our literary, political, and social heritage; it is itself great literature and a great record of social and political events. About this we shall say more in later chapters when we trace the outlines of the world of the Bible and the way in which it came to be written. It should, however, be noted here that it is a whole library in itself. The word "Bible" is derived from the Greek *biblion,* a piece of papyrus containing some writing, and the Bible consists of sixty-six books. However, throughout the sixty-six runs the continuous theme of man's encounter with God, giving it a unity not found in most libraries.

Here in the Bible is history, not always accurate in its details, for as one may expect, where there are several accounts of the same event or when the story was written down many years after the event occurred, occasionally inconsistencies crept in. Nevertheless, it is a fascinating history of the life and thought of a great people over a period of twelve hundred years of decisive human events. It is the record of God's progressive revelation of himself to these people through everchanging and often painful situations. This history consists, for the most part, of narratives within which are to be found sharply delineated character sketches. But it is enlivened also by wonderfully imaginative folklore, riddles, oracles, and fables.

The Bible is not all history; it contains also great poetry. Some of this poetry was written to celebrate great events, for example, the very early "Song of Miriam"[19] and the "Song of Deborah"[20] in the Old Testament, which were victorious war chants, and the "Magnificat"[21] of Mary in the New Testament uttered when she learned that she was to be the mother of Jesus. We have great devotional hymns in the Book of Psalms. There is stirring nature poetry in certain psalms that acclaim God's creation and vivid description of God's mighty acts in the Book of Job.[22] Other strains of poetry have great search-

---

[19] Exod. 15:1-18
[20] Judg. 5
[21] Luke 1:46-55

[22] Cf. Pss. 8, 19, 29, 93, 104·
Job 38—41

ing depths of promise and of duty, such as the servant songs of the Book of Isaiah.[23] There is infinite sadness in the dirge of Lamentations and some parts of Jeremiah; there is fiery invective joined with a sense of righteousness and of hope in the words of Amos, the shepherd of Tekoa. History, poetry, and preaching meet in the voices of the prophets, whose utterances because of their ethical insights and spiritual discernment are to be classed among the greatest words in the Bible.

Poetry merges with philosophy in the Book of Job, which dramatically probes the problem of evil and comes out, not with a solution, but with spiritual mastery through recognition of the power of the Almighty. The Book of Proverbs consists of homely adages then current, and many of them, because of their shrewdness, are current still. The Book of Ecclesiastes, influenced by Greek thought in the later period of Israel's history, has a strongly Epicurean strain which is out of step with the main emphases in the Bible, but it contains some descriptive passages of haunting loveliness.[24]

The Bible has gripping short stories, such as the beautiful account of Ruth's fidelity and the dramatic story of Queen Esther. Jesus was a master of the storytelling art, and his parables pack more meaning into an incident than any other stories ever told. There are lighter notes also in the Bible. Jonah is an allegory with a deep meaning. The Song of Solomon is a charming love lyric, perhaps a collection of songs used at weddings.

In the New Testament the type of literature is quite different from most of what precedes it. Here the prevailing

---

[23] Cf. Isa. 42, 49, 52, 53
[24] As for example, Eccles. 3:1-11 and 12:1-7

structure is narrative with important sayings interspersed in the story, as in the four Gospels and the Book of Acts. Here are to be found both sermons and biography. A large part of the New Testament consists of letters to the churches. They were written before anything else in the New Testament and are by far the most important letters ever written. From them we learn a great deal, not only about the Christian faith, but also about Paul, who wrote most of them, and about conditions in the early Church. Then the Bible comes to a close with a cryptic but highly dramatic book—the Book of Revelation. It was born out of persecution, and promises defeat to the enemies of Christ but a new heaven and a new earth to the faithful. In these recent years when Christians have again had to go through "dungeon, fire, and sword" for their faith, the meaning of this apocalyptic (or vision) literature has come alive to many.

THE BIBLE AS SOCIAL HISTORY

Even if one were only interested in the Bible as a record of social change he can find social history here also. It begins with its setting in a primitive nomadic society not unlike that of the Bedouins of today. As the Hebrews entered and conquered Canaan they were not only settling down to a more stable agricultural society but also doing what most conquerors do when they can—exterminating, enslaving, or exiling the former occupants of the land. We see them pass through a period of political and social turmoil when "every man did that which was right in his own eyes"[25] until the monarchy was established to ensure greater stability. It rises to great

---

[25] Judg. 21:25

power and brilliance under David, only to go down again under the extravagant display and extortion of his unwise son Solomon. We see it split apart into two kingdoms, and then they go down to defeat before the armies of the east, first the Northern and then the Southern Kingdom. We see Palestine the buffer state over which trample the armies of Egypt and Assyria as each of these powerful neighbors strives to intimidate it or to use it for her own ends.

Israel lost her independence in 586 B.C. and went into exile but gained a stronger faith through the voices of her prophets. Many of the people returned a half century later, and the nation remained in unstable equilibrium until the conquest of Palestine by Alexander the Great in 332 B.C. Persecution under the overlord Antiochus Epiphanes, which forms the framework of the Book of Daniel with its lions' den and fiery furnace, led to the outbreak of the Maccabean rebellion. After fierce fighting Israel regained her freedom, but only for a brief period, for she was annexed by Rome in Pompey's eastward march of 63 B.C. The events in the New Testament took place while Israel was a vassal of the Roman Empire. With the destruction of Jerusalem by Titus in A.D. 70, Israel as a nation collapsed. However, the history of the struggles and victories of the people, in their encounters with their enemies, and still more in their encounters with God, lives today and is immortal.

Two strains run through the Bible, both important to the sociologist or historian who wants to know how people react to circumstances and why they react as they do. One of these is the concept of a chosen people, an elect nation bound in a particular way to their God, obligated by a covenant to obey

Jehovah and sustained by the hope that if they were faithful, he would guide them, strengthen them, deliver them from their enemies. Much of the Old Testament centers in the attempts of the Hebrews to live up to the requirements of this covenant, their apostasies, God's judgments upon them, his promise of a Messiah to deliver them even in spite of their sins. In the New Testament this idea of an elect nation broadens out to take in all men as sons of the one Father, and the promise of the Messiah is fulfilled in the redeeming work of Christ.

But this particular strand of what is sometimes called "holy history" is not, of course, all that is to be looked for. The people of the Bible, like any other people, wanted economic security and national prestige, got jealous of foreign groups and often of each other, connived for political or economic or personal advantage. Their acts were sometimes astute and sometimes foolish. They had some leaders who were wise and magnanimous but many who were stupid and ruthless. They loved and hated; they married and raised families, often with bickering among the children. Polygamy was common in the period covered by the early Old Testament, but had passed out of practice by the New Testament era. Not a little racial tension is evident, including manifestations of anti-Semitism such as persist to our own day. All this is fascinating material to one who is interested in human motives and group reactions to changing circumstances.

One must go to the Bible, therefore, if he wishes to understand the backgrounds of our Hebrew-Christian tradition. The Western world as we have it today did not come out of a vacuum. While it received from Greek and Roman sources an important stream of influence which the Bible scarcely touches, it also rests on foundations in which both the events and the religious convictions recorded in the Bible have a very large place. To be ignorant of the Bible is to have a blind spot to much that any educated, as well as any religious, person ought to have acquaintance with as part of his very being.

The Bible as God's Word

We have seen that the Bible is a very human book, in the sense that it deals throughout with the experiences of people and with the widest possible range of these experiences. The Bible is not a textbook on science, for it was written many centuries before the modern scientific method and the vast accumulation of facts we call scientific knowledge had been dreamed of. But with this important exception, the Bible contains reflections of every human interest—not only religion, but also history, philosophy, poetry, drama, great addresses, stories, letters, law-making, the struggles of war, the pursuits of peace. Even rather dry "vital statistics" in the form of long genealogies (for the Hebrews had a great interest in family backgrounds), census records, military rosters, and other matters which today have only an antiquarian interest, such as the dimensions of Noah's ark or Solomon's temple, appear in it. In short, though there are great gaps we wish had been filled in, such as the events of the childhood and youth of Jesus, the Bible contains every sort of thing which the people were interested in and thought important enough to write down. And to an amazing degree, its themes are the things we are interested in today.

What Is "The Word of God"?

But though the Bible is a very human book, it is also a divine book. By common consent the Church for centuries has called it the Word of God. The Bible does not call itself that, for it reserves this term for the message or revelation of God spoken to the prophets and apostles, while in the New Testament the word is "the Word made flesh" to dwell among us as the incarnate Lord. In the Old Testament, for example, we are told that Samuel asked Saul to hear the word of God before he anointed him king, and that the word of God came to Nathan to tell David not to build the temple he had projected. There is no suggestion here of the use of Scripture, for the Bible was itself only in the process of being created.

In the Gospel of John we have the most forthright and vivid use of the term, for its author, who was probably a Gentile Christian familiar with the Greek idea of the *Logos*,[26] begins his writing with the great affirmation, "In the beginning was the Word, and the Word was with God, and the Word was God." This majestic passage comes to a climax in the fourteenth verse, "And the Word became flesh, and dwelt among us (and we beheld his glory, glory as of the only begotten from the Father), full of grace and truth."[27]

Even though the Bible does not call itself the Word of God,

[26] The word *Logos*, which holds a central place in Stoic philosophy, can be translated Word but this does not do justice to its full meaning. No single term in English is its exact equivalent. *Logos* means an immanent, creative world force, a principle of reason and order that pervades all things and binds them together in a concrete unity. It is sometimes rendered World-Reason or World-Soul or World-Spirit. Christian thought in identifying the Logos with Christ gave it a more personal meaning than it had in Greek thought.

[27] A.S.V.

it is a legitimate metaphor for us to use, provided it is rightly understood. The word of God means "God speaking," God declaring himself, God making known to his hearers his will and way. The author of the Epistle to the Hebrews caught its meaning with great accuracy when he opened his letter with the words:

> In many and various ways God spoke of old to our fathers by the prophets; but in these last days he has spoken to us by a Son. . . . He reflects the glory of God and bears the very stamp of his nature, upholding the universe by his word of power.[28]

This is to say that the same God who spoke through the prophets has spoken with greater clarity, vividness, and power through his Son. God's Word, then, means God's self-disclosure.

Applied to the Bible, this conception of the Word as God's self-disclosure affords great assurance but also interposes a very necessary caution. Let us see, therefore, what we must do—and must not do—if the Bible is to be the Word of God to us.

How To Hear the Word

In the first place, it is essential that one's mind and spirit be alert to hear what God says. When a woman tries to call her family to meals and they are so bent on their own pursuits that they do not come, or tries to correct a child who pays no attention, or talks into the telephone to discover suddenly that she has been cut off or that the other party has hung up the receiver, she is not really speaking to anyone.

---

[28] Heb. 1:1-3, R.S.V.

Try as best she may, if there is no response she is not disclosing anything to anybody but simply talking into the air. This baffling experience, which everybody has now and then, can perhaps suggest how God yearns to communicate far more important messages than any of us ever have to give, but is unable to do so except to receptive persons.

From the human point of view, such unreceptiveness automatically cuts off the possibility that the Bible can be the Word of God to us. It can be studied with the best of critical scholarship, such as we all need in order to understand it most fully. Historical criticism is quite compatible with warm appreciation, and to be a biblical critic does not imply anything adverse any more than it does to be a music critic or literary critic, who would be useless unless he had the capacity for appreciating what is good in his field. But unless the Bible is read in faith, which means not in naive credulity but in personal responsiveness, it falls short of being the Word of God to the reader.

This points up the necessity of taking to the Bible a teachable mind. This means using the best available tools of scholarship and being willing if necessary to give up cherished former ideas if new truth appears. God cannot speak to closed or biased minds. If, for example, we have been in the habit of thinking of God's total creation of the world as occurring in six days of twenty-four hours each and we learn that the creation stories in Genesis are a prescientific attempt to present great religious truth rather than accurate geology or biology, we fail to hear God speak if we refuse to change our minds.

But to hear God speak requires, even more necessarily, a devout mind. The Bible's supreme message of God's love for sinners and his eagerness to give new life and power to the repentant one who responds to the Father's love, breaks through all bonds to reach any who will hear and heed it. It is significant that from the second century to the nineteenth, when modern historical scholarship became current, theories about the Bible were held which no competent historian now accepts, such as that Moses wrote the entire Pentateuch (the first five books of the Old Testament) including the description of his own death. Yet during all this time, and particularly after the Protestant Reformation had drawn the focus away from the Church to the Bible as the channel of God's self-disclosure, people kept on being nourished by it and led by it to Christlike lives. This is to say—not that biblical scholarship and the correction of errors can be unimportant but rather—that the one indispensable thing, if the Bible is to be the Word of God, is a receptive attitude of spirit and responsiveness of will.

We ought therefore to read the Bible critically, analytically, and with as full an understanding as we can get of its historical setting, its types of literature, the conditions under which it was written, and the motives that prompted its characters in living and its authors in writing it. Some suggestion of this we shall give in outline form in the next chapters, though for any full understanding we ought to consult larger books such as those listed in the bibliography. But while doing this, as a lifetime practice, we ought to read the Bible devotionally, accompanying it with prayer, waiting before it in quietness and with self-examination to see what God is saying to us through it. Unless we do this we are likely, on the one hand, to fall into a barren and sterile pedantry as we try to dissect it, or on the other to become dogmatic and intolerant toward those who have interpretations differing from our own.

However, it is not enough simply to read the Bible receptively, for we may err in what we receive from it. People in full sincerity have sometimes picked verses here and there, thought that they read in them the utterance of God, and have tried to justify their own impulses to slander or slaughter their fellow men. For example, take the phrase, "Vengeance is mine; I will repay, saith the Lord," in Romans 12:19. This has been used more than once to justify wreaking vengeance on one's enemies who, because they are God's enemies, must be put down by God's servants. Taken in its context—with "Avenge not yourselves, but rather give place unto wrath" preceding, and "Therefore, if thine enemy hunger, feed him: if he thirst, give him drink" immediately following—it is evident that the exact opposite is intended. An even more dangerously perverted passage is in the first verse of the very next chapter: "The powers that be are ordained of God. Whosoever therefore resisteth the power, resisteth the ordinance of God." This has been used to justify not only a theory of the divine right of kings, but acquiescence in Naziism and other diabolical forms of political tyranny.

This makes it apparent that we must have some standard for interpreting the Bible, rejecting false renderings or unworthy concepts as not being the voice of God and accepting true ones. This is a big problem, to which in a sense this whole book is devoted. Two principles only we shall stress at this point. One has already been stated—that we must get all the historical and literary light we can on the passage to decide what it meant to the original writer, why he said it, whether it expresses permanent truth or only a passing phase of his

or his people's experience. There are a good many pronounce-
ments in the Bible, like Paul's injunctions to women not to
pray to God with their heads uncovered[29] and to keep silence
in the churches,[30] which had reasonable foundation in those
times, but not any longer. It would have been unfortunate
for the Christian Corinthian women to have been confused
with the blatant *hetairai,* the street-walkers of loose morals,
but it is equally unfortunate when such injunctions are appealed
to today to curtail the religious expression or leadership of
devoted Christian women. Although in Semitic folklore there
seemed nothing inappropriate in supposing that the first woman
was made from Adam's rib,[31] we are not obligated to take
the story literally.

There is a principle that goes deeper than the best historical
and literary criticism and which, though it never can be applied inflexibly, is our truest index. Said Paul to the Philippians,
"Let this mind be in you, which was also in Christ Jesus
. . . ."[32] Though we can never hope fully either to imitate
Christ in our living or to think as he thought, the more steadfastly we live with his personality, letting his spirit capture
us, the more assurance we can have in our ethical judgments.
The fact that a statement is found in the Bible does not make
it true. What makes it true is that it comes from God, and
our best knowledge of whether or not it is of God is whether
it accords with the life, the words, the mind of Christ. Remember, the Word of God means "God speaking," and while
we do not have in the gospel record the answers to all our
questions, the Christian believes that the Word of God comes

---

[29] I Cor. 11:13   [31] Gen. 2:21
[30] I Cor. 14:34   [32] Phil. 2:5

to man most fully, clearly, unequivocally, in Jesus Christ.

The examples cited above may be used again in illustration. Why do we question that Paul was inspired of God when he wrote, "Neither was man created for woman, but woman for man"[33]; yet respond with full assurance when we find the same writer saying, "There is neither Jew nor Greek, there is neither slave nor free, there is neither male nor female; for you are all one in Christ Jesus"[34]? The reason is that Jesus treated men and women equally as children of God and persons of supreme worth. One could hardly imagine his saying that women are created for men and not men for women, for he seems rather to say that we are all created to love and serve one another. In spite of the fact that Karl Barth in the Commission on the Life and Work of Women at the Amsterdam Conference attempted to put the relation of women to the work of the Church on the theological basis of Adam's rib and Ephesians 5:23 ("For the husband is the head of the wife as Christ is the head of the church"[35]), most of us still believe that Paul comes nearest to the mind of Christ in Galatians 3:28.

IS THE BIBLE INSPIRED?

Until now we have made little reference to a word that is likely to set off controversy wherever it is spoken, the *inspiration* of the Bible. The reason it is so often a matter of dispute is that people differ in what they mean when they use the word, and since deep emotions are tied in with the conviction that the Bible is inspired, to doubt the kind of inspiration one believes in is apt to seem like rejecting the

---

[33] I Cor. 11:9, R.S.V.   [34] Gal. 3:28, R.S.V.   [35] R.S.V.

Bible outright or making it no different from any other book. The reason we have avoided the term is not to dodge the issue, for it is a very important one, but rather to lay groundwork for trying to answer the question.

An idea which was long held, and is still held by some, is that God spoke directly through the Holy Spirit to each writer of the Bible in such a manner that the author wrote down with perfect accuracy exactly what God told him to write. This idea, which in spite of giving a place to the Holy Spirit, is based on divine dictation, is called *verbal inspiration.* It holds that the Bible is at every point infallible. On this assumption one may open it anywhere, and whatever he finds must be "gospel truth."

This view leads to a very high reverence for the Bible, and some great Christians have held it. However, it leads also to other results that are not so good. One has to gloss over the crude ethics that one finds mixed in with great moral ideals, not only in such matters as we have cited from Paul but still more in the Old Testament where God is at times represented as helping and even directing his people to steal and kill, the Ten Commandments to the contrary. It raises problems about the nature of God himself, who is not uniformly represented as the righteous, loving God of Christian faith, but sometimes as peevish, jealous, and changeable. Even if one overlooks such matters as these—and there is a tendency to overlook them by looking only at the parts of the Bible that fit better with the idea of an infallible book—there is still the matter of inconsistencies and internal self-contradictions which appear at many points. Much effort has been put forth to try to reconcile such inconsistencies, but some of them remain irreconcilable.

We shall later have occasion to note numerous illustrations of such problems as were mentioned in the preceding paragraph. We shall stop now for only one illustration. What does the Bible say about man and his destiny? Go to the Book of Ecclesiastes and you read:

> For that which befalleth the sons of men befalleth beasts; even one thing befalleth them: as the one dieth, so dieth the other; yea, they have all one breath; so that a man hath no preeminence above a beast; for all is vanity.[36]

But go to the majestic words of Paul in the fifteenth chapter of I Corinthians and you find:

> For this corruptible must put on incorruption, and this mortal must put on immortality.
> So when this corruptible shall have put on incorruption, and this mortal shall have put on immortality, then shall be brought to pass the saying that is written, Death is swallowed up in victory.
> O death, where is thy sting? O grave, where is thy victory?[37]

There is no good way of reconciling these two statements. Which is right? The fact that one has comforted and lifted many generations of Christians with a great hope, while probably not many readers of this book knew that the other was in the Bible, gives answer as to which of them is truly inspired. But if even in this one instance—to say nothing of various others which might be cited—two passages flatly

---

[36] Eccles. 3:19   [37] Cor. 15:53-55

contradict each other, they cannot both be the infallible voice of God.

Are we to say, then, that the Bible is not inspired? *By no means.* Rather, we shall have to get a different idea of what is meant by inspiration. The word *inspiration* means "in-breathing." The Bible is inspired in the sense that the in-breathing of the divine appears on every page. It is the record of the spiritual experience of a people who over the twelve centuries spanned by its writing were guided, supported, chastened, forgiven, delivered, redeemed by God. Its great theme is salvation, and centering about this theme it has a marvelous unity in spite of its discrepancies in detail. The human deficiencies, as well as the great insights, of the men who wrote it are there, but what is more important, we see God there and hear him speak through the writer's words. In the Bible we have "heavenly treasure" even though it is in "earthen vessels." What we need to do in order to grasp its meaning is to give full recognition to both elements, and the divine message will shine through with greater richness and power if we understand something of the channels of human fallibility mixed with high insights through which the message comes.

If what has been said is true, we need not be afraid to study the Bible with open eyes. Indeed, we shall need to have our eyes open very wide to catch even a small portion of its rich treasury of meaning. We shall try, therefore, in the next chapter to put ourselves as well as we can into the world in which the Bible came into being.

CHAPTER TWO

The World of the Bible

In the previous chapter we indicated something of the importance of the Bible to our culture, and traced the outlines of its literary and historical framework. The question was opened up as to what is meant by the Bible as the revealed Word of God. We shall deal further with this matter later on, but we must now examine a little more closely the setting in which the Bible was written, and thus get a better perspective of the movements through which God "visited and redeemed his people."

To do this, it will be necessary to take a glance at the kind of world—physical, psychological, and social—in which the Hebrew people lived. They lived in a very different world from ours—a world which inevitably conditioned the nature of the experiences they had and the literature they produced. The marvel is that living in so different a world, they could still say so much that today "speaks to our condition."

The Physical Setting

The biblical world, meaning that section of the earth's surface which the people of the Bible knew about or had something to do with, covers a considerable territory though still a small part of the world as we now know it. It stretches from Spain on the west to the Persian Gulf on the east; from the Black and Caspian Seas on the north to the southern end of the Red Sea. The outermost fringes of this section, however, were known only by hearsay, if at all, by most of the people of Bible times. The part of this section in which their fortunes were cast comprised Palestine at the center; the Tigris-Euphrates Valley, eastern arm of the Fertile Crescent around the Arabian desert; Egypt and the Sinai Peninsula to the southwest; and the north shore of the Mediterranean, which does not appear much in the Old Testament but was an important sphere of missionary journeys in the New. Each of these sections had a culture and, back of the culture, physical features which played a very important part in the destinies of the Hebrew people.

We shall now take a look at each of these areas. The reader is advised at this point to find a Bible that contains maps and study them, locating at least the places mentioned below. Even an elementary knowledge of biblical geography helps to make many things come alive.

PALESTINE

The land which we call Palestine (from the Philistines, who occupied much of it until the Hebrews dislodged them) is hardly ever so called in the Bible.[1] It is known rather as Canaan, or spoken of by its main divisions, the land of Israel in the north and of Judah in the south. It occupies a territory 150 miles long and 80 miles wide, about the size of the state of Vermont, and is in nearly the same latitude north of the equator as our state of Georgia. It has a very broken configura-

---

[1] There are references in Exod. 15:14 and Isa. 14:29, 31 to what is translated Palestina in the King James Version, but Philistia in the Revised Standard. Philistia itself bordered the Mediterranean.

tion, and most of the soil is poor, hard to make a living from. The Jews who have gone there in recent years have done an amazing job of applying modern methods of agriculture to make it productive, but this was not so in Bible times. It is cut through the middle, to the east of center,[2] by the Jordan River which makes a very crooked, rapid descent from Mount Hermon in the north to lose itself in the Dead Sea, 1,300 feet below sea level, east of the mountainous section where Jerusalem is situated. About one third of the way down, the Jordan spreads out to form a beautiful lake, the Sea of Galilee.

In this north central Galilee section, where Nazareth is located and Jesus spent his boyhood, are rolling hills with pleasant vineyards and olive groves. To the southwest of it, the fertile Plain of Esdraelon, tramped across by many armies, connects the Jordan area with the Mediterranean. In the central section, south of the Plain of Esdraelon, is Samaria. This was the seat of the Northern Kingdom, and the city of Samaria was its capital until it fell before the Assyrian hosts in 722 B.C. In New Testament times this section was occupied by the despised Samaritans, with whom most of the Jews had no dealings.

South of Samaria lay Judea whose capital was the holy city of Jerusalem. This is rocky, barren territory, and its people always had to struggle to make a living. In this section, about the size of Rhode Island, some of the most momentous events in the history of the world took place, including two events transcending all others—the birth and death of Jesus. Bethlehem is five miles south of Jerusalem. Down a steep road to

---

[2] The eastern boundary has varied at different times, and the section east of the Jordan is now known as Transjordania.

the northeast lies Jericho, in the fertile valley of the Jordan,
near where the river empties into the Dead Sea. The writer
remembers the hair-raising experience of "going down
from Jerusalem to Jericho" in a rattle-trap automobile which
may have had brakes but appeared to have none, and coming
out near Jericho to see luscious grapes in bunches a foot long.
To the east of Judea proper is the wilderness of Judea to which
Jesus may have withdrawn—waterless, treeless, cut by deep
gorges which made it a place of desolation. To the south of
Judea is the Negeb, another desert wilderness, which merges
to the southwest with the Sinai Peninsula where the Hebrews
lived as nomads for a considerable period after their escape
from Egypt, before they entered Palestine from the east.

Along the Mediterranean coast of Judea lay the Plain of
Philistia, for the possession of which much fighting was done.
Its cities of Gaza, Gath, Ashdod, and Ashkelon have a familiar
sound to those acquainted with the stories of Saul and Samson.
North of Philistia was the Plain of Sharon, where the port
city of Joppa was situated, and in New Testament times,
Caesarea. This plain extends from the coast to the hills of
Samaria. On Sharon's northern border, near the western end
of the great Plain of Esdraelon which stretches southeast from
the Mediterranean to the Jordan Valley, stands Mount Carmel
where the prophet Elijah had his famous contest with the
priests of Baal. Still farther north is the Plain of Acre where
the modern port of Haifa is located, and beyond Acre lay
Phoenicia with its important capital, Tyre. This wealthy commercial city, though it was never under Hebrew political control, was allied by ties of trade as well as geographical
propinquity. Modern Beirut, in Lebanon which lies to

the north of Palestine, is in the area which used to be Phoenicia
and which sent forth the first great merchant fleets to sail
the Mediterranean world.

The northernmost city of Canaan was Dan, the southern-
most Beersheba, hence the expression "from Dan to Beersheba."
When we do not want anything told, we are apt to quote from
David's lament over Saul and Jonathan,

>Tell it not in Gath,
>Publish it not in the streets of Ashkelon.[3]

The setting of Jesus' encounter with the woman at the well
becomes very clear when we read, "He left Judaea, and departed
again into Galilee. And he must needs go through Samaria,"[4]
while the Parable of the Good Samaritan gets its point from
the neighborly act of a member of a neighboring but alien
group. Statements such as,

>My soul thirsteth for thee, my flesh longeth for thee,
>In a dry and weary land, where no water is,[5]

and

>As the mountains are round about Jerusalem,
>So the Lord is round about his people,[6]

become more vivid when we see these figures of speech in
relation to the physical situation of the people who first sang
these hymns.

The physical contours of the country laid their stamp upon
its people. The people of the Southern Kingdom, in Judea,
were rugged fighters, and "men to match the mountains," at
least in physical stamina and courage, not infrequently ap-

---

[3] II. Sam. 1:20, R.S.V.
[4] John 4:3, 4
[5] Ps. 63:1, A.S.V.
[6] Ps. 125:2, R.S.V.

peared. The people of Samaria and Galilee were more pros-
perous, and inclined to be more peace-loving. The Phoenicians
were fairly shoved into the ocean by the proximity of the Lebanon mountains, while the Hebrews never took to the sea.
Then as now, the country was too small for the population,
and the *diaspora,* or dispersion, of the Jews to other lands
was caused by economic as well as political and military factors.

We now return to the geographical feature of the Holy Land
that had the greatest influence on its destiny: the strategic
location of Palestine between the great contending powers,
Assyria and Babylon to the east and Egypt to the southwest.
This meant that Israel was a buffer state between them, whose
possession was eagerly sought by strong neighbors as a step
toward larger prey. Much of Israel's political history is written in terms of attempts by force of arms, diplomacy, or tribute
money to keep her independence. But this location also meant
that a great caravan route, the only feasible way to get past
the Arabian desert, lay across her territory. This greatly in-
creased cultural penetration in a day when travel was difficult
and there were no newspapers or radios. Cultural intermingling
inevitably took place on the frontier between a nomadic society
to the south and a settled, advanced civilization to the southwest and northeast. More than she realized, Israel borrowed
from her neighbors, whose physical setting we must now examine.

THE MESOPOTAMIAN VALLEY

A story is told of a woman whose emotions were so easily
stirred that she wept "whenever she heard that blessed word
Mesopotamia." To the Hebrews the Mesopotamian section

was anything but blessed, though often the occasion of weeping. Their tears have been immortally expressed in the hymn of lament from their Exile,

> By the rivers of Babylon,
> There we sat down, yea, we wept,
> When we remembered Zion.[7]

The word Mesopotamia means "between the rivers." And between two very great rivers it is, the Tigris and the Euphrates. Rising in the highlands of Armenia and fed by mountain snows, they flow southeasterly to meet at a point seventy miles from the Persian Gulf, to which they carry much silt. The water from these two rivers redeems from barrenness land that would otherwise be desert, and creates a fertile valley from which one of the great civilizations of the ancient past emerged.

We have noted that this section is often called the Fertile Crescent. The crescent is somewhat skewed, but if one consults a topographical map, it is unmistakably there. It stretches from Palestine through Syria, through Upper Mesopotamia, which was the seat of Assyrian power, and Lower Mesopotamia, where Babylon was located, to terminate at the Persian Gulf. One of its southernmost points is Ur of the Chaldees from which, it is said, "By faith Abraham . . . went out, not knowing whither he went."[8] Situated to the south of the crescent, bounded by Palestine toward the sea and the Tigris-Euphrates Valley on the north and east, is the Arabian Desert. This section we now call the Middle East, and Iraq, prized for its oil wells, occupies the greater part of the Tigris-Euphrates Valley.

---

[7] Ps. 137:1, A.S.V.   [8] Heb. 11:8.

In Bible times, however, the oil had not been discovered nor had its commercial values been dreamed of. What the people needed most was water for themselves, their grasslands and their crops, and canals and reservoirs were developed with much engineering skill to drain off the flood waters and irrigate the land. In the northern part of the valley arose the great Assyrian Empire with its capital city at Nineveh, which one can scarcely mention without thinking of Kipling's "Recessional,"

> Lo, all our pomp of yesterday
> Is one with Nineveh and Tyre![9]

It was the Assyrian armies that conquered Samaria and put an end to the Northern Kingdom in 722 B.C. But it was not long before the center of power had begun to move southward, and it was the Babylonians, under King Nebuchadrezzar,[10] who conquered Jerusalem in 586 B.C. and took the best part of the Hebrew people into exile in Babylon. Babylonia, situated on a broad low plain between the rivers at their widest points, was very fertile and had developed an advanced culture as early as 3500 B.C. From this region comes the famous Code of Hammurabi which, dating from long before the time of Moses, shows high ethical discernment regarding the establishment of justice in human relations.

EGYPT AND THE SINAI PENINSULA

We must now look to Israel's neighbors to the southwest and the south. We shall begin with Egypt, which was the cradle of civilization in the ancient world. Primitive though much of

---

[9] Rudyard Kipling, "Recessional" (Toronto: Macmillan Co. of Canada Ltd.)

[10] Called in the Bible Nebuchadnezzar.

it now seems, it was here that "the dawn of conscience"[11] took place. The Sphinx and the Pyramids still stand, in the midst of dirt and sordidness, as monuments to a great past. Water is the key to this early greatness, for without the Nile there would have been no Egypt.

The Nile, nearly 4,000 miles long, rises just north of the equator and flows northward to empty into the Mediterranean after forming a large delta on which is situated the important city of Alexandria. The waters of the Nile never fail, for one of its tributaries, the White Nile, is fed by Lake Victoria Nyanza, the second largest lake in the world, and the other, the Blue Nile, receives the heavy summer rains from the mountains of Abyssinia. Meeting at Khartoum they create a fertile valley 10 to 30 miles wide, which is in sharp contrast to the desert of Sahara, just west of it. Along this narrow stretch of fertile land arose the great early temples at Luxor and Karnak and the great cities of Thebes, Memphis, and Cairo. In the southeastern part of the Nile delta, about halfway between Cairo and the sea, lay the land of Goshen. It was here, in all probability, that the Hebrew people were in bondage to the Pharoahs until by the hand of God, under the leadership of Moses, they escaped across the Bitter Lakes (north of the main part of the Gulf of Suez and a long way north of the Red Sea) to begin their wilderness wanderings.

These wanderings were not, as the term might suggest, simply an aimless attempt to find the way out of the wilderness. Rather, the people, who were shepherds, lived as nomads in the Sinai Peninsula, pasturing their flocks and moving from place to place as the need for pasturage demanded. They eked out a

---

[11] Note Professor J. H. Breasted's excellent book by this title.

bare living, and it is no wonder that they sometimes longed for "the fleshpots of Egypt" and again felt very grateful to God for some unexpected deliverance from hunger. The peninsula is triangular in shape, bounded on the southwest by the Gulf of Suez and on the southeast by the Gulf of Akabah. It was formerly thought that Mount Sinai, where Moses is said to have received the Ten Commandments, lay to the south near the apex of this triangle, but it is now more generally believed to have been in the east in the Mount Seir Range north of the Gulf of Akabah. In any case, the people must have worked their way across this wide expanse of the Sinai Peninsula and northward to Moab which is east of the Dead Sea, then after Moses' death, still farther northward to where they could cross the Jordan near Jericho.

THE NORTH MEDITERRANEAN WORLD

The land north of the Mediterranean is very different from the scene just noted. Nevertheless, it is part of the biblical world, and in the days of the founding of the early Church, it was a very important part.

North of Palestine lay Syria.[12] In Bible times Syria had two very important cities, Damascus and Antioch. Damascus, a great trading center on the western border of the Fertile Crescent, is a very ancient city—perhaps the oldest anywhere in the world which still exists—while Antioch is famous for the fact that here the followers of Christ were first called Christians. One cannot go much farther north than Antioch without bumping into the Taurus Mountains, the watershed that separates

---

[12] Ancient Syria contained what is now both Syria and Lebanon, and modern Beirut is in Lebanon.

the Euphrates Valley from Asia Minor and hence the Orient from the Occident. There is a pass near the northeast corner of the Mediteranean, just south of which is the city of Tarsus where Paul grew up. The Romans were great roadbuilders, and in the first century a highway ran from Ephesus, the principal city on the Aegean coast, through Antioch in Pisidia, Iconium, Lystra, Derbe, and Tarsus, to Antioch in Syria. It is easy therefore to see why Paul chose the route he did when he traveled inland to carry the gospel, though we are not to suppose that even on the best highway the times afforded he traveled in the comfort of a Ford car. Aside from the sea journeys we are not told what conveyance he and the others used in their travels abroad preaching the gospel, but it is probable that for the most part they walked and rode donkeyback.

And a long way, for those times, they traveled, for north of the Aegean Sea lies Macedonia, the main cities of which were Philippi, Thessalonica, and Berea. All these received visits; and letters to the churches that were founded in two of them gave names to books of the New Testament. The two main cities of Greece were Athens, the center of philosophy, art, and culture, and Corinth, a wealthy and inclined-to-be-wicked city at the isthmus which connects the Peloponnesus with the mainland. Paul reached both of these, and the Corinthian church became one of his chief joys and headaches. He knew about Spain, and in a letter to the church at Rome said that he planned to visit them on the way to Spain, which he never reached. Apparently he was imprisoned at Rome during the persecutions under Nero and there gave up his life for his faith. His last letter, written from prison to the church at Philippi, is rich with wise counsel and spiritual victory in the conviction that "to live is Christ, and to die is gain."

The Social Setting of the Old Testament

Even more briefly we must now take a glance at the social situations reflected in the Bible, pausing to comment only on those features most essential to its understanding.

The social setting did not, of course, remain static during the long period covered by Bible history. Certain elements, however, remained fairly common throughout. Among these are the central place of the family in social organization, the inferior status of women in the household (though not so low as in many other Oriental cultures), the sharp lines of cleavage drawn between the Hebrews and all other peoples whether enemies or simply neighboring groups, the intense conviction that their social and political fortunes were bound up with their religious status and destiny.

OCCUPATIONS

Shepherds.—Hebrew history begins, as has been intimated, in nomadic life. Whether authentic history is taken to begin with the migrations of Abraham from Ur of the Chaldees or in the exodus from Egypt under the leadership of Moses, our first real picture of the Hebrews is as a group of shepherds trying to find pasturage for their flocks. With the tendency of the biblical writers to regard all events as coming directly from the hand of God, the economic forces which apparently led to these migrations take on a religious coloring. This appears in such vividly told stories as the separation of Abraham and Lot because their herdsmen quarreled, Jacob's journey eastward to

Haran to get a wife from among his mother's people and his long service in tending the flocks of his uncle Laban, the famine that sent Jacob's other sons to Egypt for food when Joseph had become Pharaoh's overlord. Reflected in these stories is a picture of patriarchal society with the father of the household the dominant head of the clan, and with few friendly dealings with neighboring clans.

With the exodus from Egypt, society continued to be nomadic. But with a difference. It was the genius of Moses, one of the world's great statesmen, that organized a group of loosely related clans into a nation and inspired the people with a new sense of their national destiny under divine law and leadership. Whether or not the story of the giving of the Ten Commandments on Mount Sinai amid thunder and lightning and great pictorial drama is to be taken literally, there is little question that the Hebrews entered Canaan with a clearer sense both of their covenant relation to their deity and of their moral and social obligations to each other than they had possessed prior to Moses' leadership.

Warriors.—The entrance into Canaan is marked by two vitally important changes. In the first place the Hebrews, in order to conquer the land, were forced to become a warlike people. If they were going to live there at all, they had to overcome the former occupants who naturally resented their intrusion. This period of conquest gave opportunity for a series of warlords, called in the Bible "judges," to seize power and become local despots, without any central authority to unite the people. Things were pretty crude and cruel in those days.

Farmers.—The second great change that came with the entrance into Canaan was the shift from a nomadic to an agricultural society. There were no longer great open spaces in which to keep moving from place to place. The Canaanites before them were farmers, and farmers the Hebrews had to become. From this fact arose all sorts of legal provisions—prohibitions against removing one's neighbor's landmark (there were no surveyors with compasses in those days or recorded deeds of landholdings), injunctions to bring the first fruits of the land as a gift to God, provisions for observing the harvest festivals, ordinances as to slaves and "the stranger within the gates." A more serious result of this shift to an agricultural society was the tendency to adopt the Canaanite (and before that, Babylonian) fertility cults of Baal and Ashtoreth, and to forsake the worship of Yahweh for a deity they thought might be more economically useful to them by increasing their herds and crops. Against this tendency the prophets had repeatedly to protest.

Tradesmen.—Agriculture, primitive in its methods till very recent times, has remained the chief occupation of the people of Palestine. There were, of course, smiths and traders of various sorts, as well as a large group of the priesthood. But the Jews had to leave Palestine, later on, in the "dispersion" to Babylon, to Alexandria, and then to the world, to become the commercial people they have notably been through the centuries. There is more than an accidental connection between the national homelessness of Jews through twenty centuries and the trading acumen for which, according to one's mood, they may either be praised or criticized. The next time you buy something of the Jewish merchant down the street, remember that if Palestine had been big and fertile, like the plains of our Middle West or a Southern plantation, in all probability the Jews would have

stayed there instead of becoming enterprising, and often persecuted, wanderers over the face of the earth.

GOVERNMENT

Monarchy.—The other aspect of the conquest period—the
tendency to disunion under petty tyrants—could not last, or
the Hebrew people would soon have perished in civil war or
become prey to their powerful neighbors. As we noted in
Chapter One, the period of the judges was followed by the monarchy which meant more political cohesion, though it was soon
to be cohesion around two centers instead of one. The twelve
tribes were divisions of the people under the assumption of a
common ancestry in Abraham, Isaac, and Jacob and then in
Jacob's twelve sons. Such lineal descent was doubtless more as-
sumed than actual, for geographical propinquity entered into
the constituency of the tribes. But this framework made it
possible for the people to hold together, first with all the Hebrews under one king, then with the ten tribes of the Northern
Kingdom under one monarch and the tribes of Judah and Ben-
jamin to the south under another.

Under the monarchy the rich became richer and the poor
became poorer. This tendency is, of course, always latent in
any social organization, but became overt and acute at this period
of Israel's history. As we saw earlier, the contrast was enhanced
by the glitter and display and magnificent building programs
of some of the monarchs who exacted hard labor and heavy
taxes from the people. It was almost constantly accented by the
need of military defense and tribute money to stave off their
strong and covetous neighbors. Parallels with our own day are
not difficult to find. Parallels continue in the matter of a great

deal of drunkenness, licentiousness, and secularism on the one hand, and on the other, internal bickerings among the leaders as to the best policy of protection from their enemies.

It was a combination of such internal weakness and outer attack that led to the eventual collapse of both kingdoms. The Northern Kingdom never recovered. The Assyrian king who conquered it scattered large numbers of the inhabitants all over his other realms, where they became the "ten lost tribes" of Israel.[18] To fill their places he imported colonists from other parts of his kingdom, who married with those who were left and formed the mixed-breed Samaritans of the New Testament. The destiny of the Hebrews continues onward through the people of the Southern Kingdom, who after their exile in Babylon returned in considerable numbers, though not as a whole, to resettle Jerusalem and its environs and rebuild the Temple as the center of their faith and fortunes.

Exile.—The Exile was of profound significance in the history of the Hebrews. Religiously, it meant that the faithful among them, though lamenting their absence from Zion, discovered that they could worship God in a strange land. The messages of Ezekiel and the Second Isaiah were delivered against this background.[14] The emergence of the synagogue as a substitute for the Temple as the place of worship occurred in this era. After their return, the priests had a much stronger influence than before, and the great ideals of the prophets were in large measure lost sight of. The Exile marks, therefore, both a

---

[18] The contention of the present Anglo-Israelites that the ten lost tribes reached England has, therefore, no historical foundation.

[14] Some Old Testament scholars think that the message of the Second Isaiah, beginning with chap. 40, was written in exile while others date it later.

broadening and a narrowing of the Hebrews' religious outlook.

The Exile had also an important cultural influence. For the first time, the Jews who were carried to Babylon were exposed to a fertile country where they found wealth, art, culture, and ample commercial opportunities. Many of them liked it and did not care to go back. Others who had fled to Egypt to avoid being deported found there also a congenial home. In both places they seem to have been reasonably well treated and given much freedom. This period marks therefore the beginning of the scattering (*diaspora*) of the Jews and the shift, for many of them, from an agricultural to a commercial way of life.

But what of those who returned? Not all the inhabitants had left, for those deported were chiefly "the better element," the ruling class and artisans. There were numerous problems of adjustment between the poorer settlers who had been left behind and those who came back. After twenty years they got the Temple rebuilt, but it was at least a century and a half before, under the vigorous governorship of Nehemiah, they rebuilt the city wall and restored Jerusalem enough to make it habitable. From then on Judea was a small, semiautonomous state with the holy city as its center. Its fortunes after Alexander's conquest and later as a Roman province have already been noted.

The Social Setting of the New Testament

A brief word must be said about the social setting of the New Testament. Palestine in the time of Jesus had largely a peasant society. It consisted mainly of small farmers and, near the sea of Galilee, of fishermen, with artisans like carpenters and tanners, with enough shepherds to make the symbols of the lost sheep and the good shepherd meaningful, and with small-town merchants to provide for the exchange of the few goods needed to meet the simple requirements of the people. It was occupied territory. There was little wealth, and most of what existed was in the hands of the tax-collectors and other foreign officials.

The priests, and in particular the high priests, had much power. The Sadducees, aristocrats who wished to stand in with the Roman authorities, were probably in most cases well-to-do as well as influential, for they controlled the temple worship and hence the temple riches. Their rivals, the Pharisees, strict champions of the Mosaic law, like the scribes who were its official interpreters, had much ecclesiastical, though less of temporal, authority.

The common people accepted as a matter of course the control of these political and religious groups, save for chronic grumblings against those who touched their pocketbooks most directly, the hated publicans or tax-collectors. While many longed for the restoration of Judah to its former glory and sighed hopefully for a political messiah to sit again on the throne of David, the Zealots who wished to throw off the Roman yoke by violent revolution were a relatively small group. Slavery was the accepted practice, though there is little evidence of its grosser features. Debt and harsh measures to collect the debt were common. The Jews had no dealings with the Samaritans. In short, the Palestine of Jesus' day was a mildly stratified, largely rural, society in which are to be discerned all the familiar social forces of political and ecclesiastical dominance, religious formalism, extremes of poverty and wealth, economic insecurity, racial cleavage, an acceptance of the *status quo* with mixed reactions of acquiescence and revolt. While Jesus' world was in some respects very primitive in comparison with today's, in its fundamental temptations to the human spirit it was amazingly like ours.

The Religious Setting

The most noteworthy aspect of the religious setting of Hebrew history is the presence of two tendencies, apparently contradictory, yet actually synthesized and running jointly throughout. These are the tendencies to take on the religious coloring of the times and to make of their experience something new and unique in human history.

One sees these tendencies in the extent to which early Hebrew religion resembles primitive religion elsewhere, yet has distinctive features of its own. It does not begin in monotheism, but rather in henotheism, a form of polytheism which assumes the existence of other gods but holds that there is a particular relationship with their own. Their god Yahweh (usually translated Jehovah, though less accurately) had entered into a covenant with them, they believed. It is this covenant that kept the Hebrews a deeply religious people through many temptations and apostasies, and enabled them in the midst of much that is primitive to keep looking higher.

There is a good deal of animism about early Hebrew religion; that is, the Hebrews believed that spirits dwelt in such inanimate objects as trees, springs, wells, stones, and mountains. Doubtless many of their "sacred places" were adopted by the Hebrews from tribes whom they dispossessed. But to them such natural phenomena as the oaks where Abraham met God[15] or the

---

[15] Gen. 12:6 ff; 18:1 R.S.V.

burning bush where Moses heard God speak[16] had a special sanctity. Stones were often set up after some great event like Jacob's vision at Bethel[17] or Joshua's leading of the people across the Jordan,[18] not only as commemorative monuments but also as shrines.

Good spirits, in the form of angels of Yahweh, came to visit men. But so did evil spirits, a host of them, as in Saul's seizure which the boy David soothed by his playing of the harp[19] and in the large numbers of demon-possessed persons whom Jesus healed. It was believed that God spoke to people in dreams, as in Jacob's dream,[20] on which is based the beautiful Negro spiritual, "We Are Climbing Jacob's Ladder." Less credible was the widespread belief that the will of God or the truth of a situation could be discerned by the Urim and Thummim, that is, by the casting of lots.[21] And still less attractive are vestiges of witchcraft, as in Saul's visit to the witch of Endor, who, according to the story, called up for him the spirit of the deceased Samuel.[22]

There is not a little magic mixed in with Hebrew religion. A good example of imitative magic is seen in the case of Moses' putting a brass serpent on a pole so that the people being bitten by serpents could be healed by looking up at it.[23] There is transfer magic also in the idea of the scapegoat, by which the sins of the people were loaded onto a goat that was then sent off into the wilderness.[24] That the Christian faith could make these primitive acts symbolic of the most holy of all relationships, the death of Christ for our redemption, is evidence of

[16] Exod. 3:1-5   [19] I Sam. 16:23   [22] I Sam. 28:3-19
[17] Gen. 28:10-22   [20] Gen. 28:12   [23] Num. 21:4-9
[18] Josh. 4:1-9   [21] Deut. 33:8, I Sam. 14:41, 42   [24] Lev. 16:20-22

the spiritual vitality of our religion. In similar vein, the blood covenant was originally a desert rite for uniting two parties by sprinkling some of an animal's blood—the seat of life—on both. When sprinkled on the altar and on the worshipers, blood became to the Hebrews a symbol of their sacred covenant with Yahweh.[25] This idea, given a deep Christian meaning, survives in the belief that the blood of Christ saves us from sin.

The Hebrews were not idolaters, except as they fell into idolatry through apostasy from their faith through Canaanite influence and had to be rebuked for it. But there is fetishism in the teraphim, or household gods, which Rachel stole when she left her father's house and sat upon for safekeeping.[26] The ark of the covenant, the most revered emblem of the Hebrew religion which was carried with them in their travels and later placed in the Holy of Holies in the Temple, also takes on the nature of a fetish when we read of its being carried into battle and bringing good luck to the Hebrews and bad luck to the Philistines who seized it.[27] Taboo, the aversion to touching anything very holy or unclean, is another aspect of early religion and culture. This too is illustrated by the ark, which no profane hands could touch, for when Uzzah attempted to steady it on its journey, he fell down dead.[28]

Enough has been said to suggest how deeply the religion of the Hebrews was enmeshed with the beliefs and practices of other early nomadic and agricultural peoples. The glory of our Hebrew-Christian faith is that from such crude beginnings so much that is high and glorious has come.

It will be necessary to leave till later any detailed tracing of

[25] Exod. 24:1-8
[26] Gen. 31:19, 30-35
[27] I Sam. 5
[28] I Chron. 13:9, 10

the growth of the Hebrew religion, and its culmination in the insights of the prophets and still higher insights of Jesus. It should be evident that God was moving in the experience of these Semitic people, leading, teaching, strengthening, chastening, inspiring them. Everything that happened, including their sufferings and some things that we should call their sins, they attributed to God's hand. Their upward climb to a sublime ethical monotheism and a Christian faith in redemption through the love of "the God and Father of our Lord Jesus Christ," gives evidence enough that in the Bible is the record of God's progressive self-disclosure.

There is much rich truth in the Bible that one misses unless he sees it as God's long process of working in wisdom and love with his people. It simply cannot be read as all on one level without losing sight of the ups and downs, which on the whole are ups, by which the people rose and fell and rose again in their discernment of God and obedience to his will. Though it is right to say that we find in the Bible the progressive revelation of God, it might be more accurate to say that the Bible shows how patiently and mercifully God always works with men, adapting his instruction to the ever-changing panorama of human experience. It shows likewise how human beings, weak and fallible and often sinful—pretty poor material at times, it seems—could persist in the quest for God and goodness. This gives us guidance and hope. Because we have the Bible, we can know what for our time and every time is the Way, the Truth, and the Life.

CHAPTER THREE

How the Old Testament Was Written

As one reads a book in its finished form, he is apt to assume that the author just began at the beginning and wrote it straight through. Occasionally an author does this. But more often, as he revises the manuscript he is apt to put in some things, pull out others, and change the order. It need not surprise us, therefore, to find that what stands first in the Bible was by no means written first.

This process of moving the parts about is even more likely to take place if what is being produced is not the product of one pen but is a symposium, the work of a number of persons. The editor not only has the job of selecting the persons who write, but also of arranging the sequence of their productions and, if necessary, of rejecting some contributions and substituting others. He has to see that in its finished form the book reads as smoothly and connectedly as possible, although symposiums seldom do succeed in having the unity of a book written by one person.

What we have in the Bible is a symposium—and a very extensive one, though without the conscious human planning one might infer from the term. It contains sixty-six books written over many hundreds of years by a great number of writers, the names of whom we know in only a relatively small number of cases. There was no single editor, although there were editors whom we call redactors who from time to time took the existing material and worked it over to form a connected story. Some of this material was in written fragments, but much of it had been preserved by telling and retelling in the oral tradition. There was relatively little writing in those days, not because the people did not know how to write, for a good many of them did, using the old Semitic alphabet script in Old Testament times and Greek in the New. But there was no printing press and no paper as we know it, and the parchment rolls on which the writing was done was a scarce commodity. Although these animal skins were more durable than most of our paper, they were perishable, for there were then no safety vaults or glass-covered museum cabinets in which to preserve them. The marvel of it is, not that there are inconsistencies and inaccuracies in the Bible as we have it, but that we have the Bible at all.

For about a hundred years Old and New Testament scholars have been working on problems of date, authorship, and sequence of the various books and parts of books. There is a large measure of agreement, which we shall draw on in this brief summary. There is not full agreement, and unless new evidence comes to light, such as the important Dead Sea Scrolls, containing among other things the text of the Book of Isaiah, which were discovered in 1947, differences of opinion are likely to continue. Scholars do not agree, for instance, as to whether the Book of Ephesians was written by Paul as traditionally supposed or by some other hand. Most New Testament students think that the Fourth Gospel, showing as it does clear traces of Greek influence, could not have been written by John the beloved disciple, but what John did write it—if, indeed, his name was John at all—is less certain. We shall not dwell much in this chapter on these doubts and uncertainties, though where necessary we shall recognize them, but will try to present what in general is a common consensus among those who have devoted their lives to the study of the Bible's structure.

History Then and Now

Both in getting at the probable sequence of the writing of history in the Bible and in passing judgment on its accuracy, some fundamental differences between the point of view of the biblical writers and of those who write history today must be kept in mind. To be a good historian according to our present standards, one must have the capacity to see the interplay of human and physical factors that caused important events to take place, and if the history is to be widely read the historian must have a clear and vivid literary style. He must be an interpreter as well as a chronicler, for lists of events with their dates are only the bare bones of history. But above all else, good historical writing must be credible; that is, it must have objective, factual accuracy as well as the historian's interpretation. The moment he begins to stretch the facts to prove a point or to tell a good story from his imagination, at that moment he becomes a propagandist or perhaps a historical novelist, but he ceases to be a true historian.

A closely related characteristic of history writing today, which comes out of our general scientific climate, is to be very wary of miracle stories. Marvelous things indeed one may relate, and must relate if there is sufficient evidence that the things to be recorded really happened. For example, the history of technological progress in the past hundred years is full of amazing things that would have seemed miraculous, if not incredible, in an earlier day. But the scientific historian tends to look for natural explanations of such events. In tracing the relations of psychological and physical factors he may have to admit that something happens which has no precedent and for which there is no ready-made explanation. Nevertheless, he still believes that it falls within an orderly system of cause and effect, and even a devoutly Christian historian is not apt to trace an event *solely* to a supernatural or miraculous act of God.

In both these respects much of the history writing in the Bible is radically different from today's. The dominant motif that characterizes all of it, as it does the whole Bible, is God's encounter with men. The biblical writers were untroubled by many of the questions we raise; they were simply narrating what they believed to be true about God's continuous activity in history. And since they lived in a prescientific age, when anything —naturally caused or otherwise—could happen, they did not hesitate to relate events as having supernatural causes.

Noting this fact, one may be tempted to throw out the history in the Bible and dismiss it as simply "unhistorical material" or "legendary tales." But to do this would be as serious an error as to take all of it as literally accurate fact. There is truth of great vitality and power in many passages of which the strictly historical accuracy may be questioned. It is our job, therefore, to find the truth that may be buried under some layers of legend.

Old Testament History

THE EARLIEST HISTORICAL RECORDS

The earliest history in the Bible recorded by a contemporary is that which tells the stories of Samuel, Saul, and David, who lived about 1000 B.C. King David had both a secretary and a recorder,[1] and it is probable that court annals were kept which enabled somebody, either in David's lifetime or almost immediately afterward, to tell in remarkably vivid and vital form the story of the powerful but frustrated and jealous Saul, his winsome and gallant son Jonathan, and the great King David. The story is told with swift, incomparably deft strokes which indicate not only what happened but why things happened as they did. Contrast, for example, the pictures of David's rise to favor with Saul and his decline:

> And Saul sent to Jesse, saying, Let David, I pray thee, stand before me; for he hath found favor in my sight. And it came to pass, when the evil spirit from God was upon Saul, that David took an harp, and played with his hand: so Saul was refreshed, and was well, and the evil spirit departed from him.[2]

But this favor was not destined to continue. After Saul had set David over his men of war, and "it was good in the sight of all the people, and also in the sight of Saul's servants," this happened:

> And it came to pass as they came, when David returned from the slaughter of the Philistine, that the women

[1] II Sam. 8:16, 17
[2] I Sam. 16:22, 23

came out of all the cities of Israel, singing and dancing, to meet king Saul, with timbrels, with joy, and with instruments of music. And the women sang one to another as they played, and said,

> Saul hath slain his thousands,
> And David his ten thousands.

And Saul was very wroth, and this saying displeased him; and he said, They have ascribed unto David ten thousands, and to me they have ascribed but thousands: and what can he have more but the kingdom? And Saul eyed David from that day and forward.[3]

This series of stories, which begins with the eighth chapter of I Samuel and runs through II Samuel into I Kings, is not only vividly written, but it also conforms in large measure to the canons of good history today. It is straightforward, unbiased narrative very largely free from miraculous explanations of events. Its best portions are the account of David's reign, extending from II Samuel 9 through I Kings 2, in which the great king's weaknesses as well as points of strength become clearly evident. This writing is the more remarkable from the fact that its unknown author was blazing a new trail, for it is excellent prose from both a historical and a literary standpoint, with no predecessor in the literature of any nation up to that time to serve as a pattern.

The story continues in I and II Kings with accounts of the reign of Solomon and his successors as the kingdom split apart under his unwise son Rehoboam, who when asked to lighten the people's load insolently replied, "My father chastised you with whips, but I will chastise you with scorpions."[4] What fol-

---

[3] I Sam. 18:6-9, A.S.V.   [4] I Kings 12:11, R.S.V.

lows is valuable history but is apparently from other hands than those of the Saul and David stories. The style is less picturesque, and the narrative follows a more formal plan: naming a king, giving a brief account of what he did, and closing with censure or praise. Since it systematically censures the northern kings and praises those of the south, it was apparently written or compiled by someone partial to the Southern Kingdom, and since this process continues over a four-hundred-year period ending with the Exile, the chances are that somebody near that time worked over the court records and put his own interpretation on them. Numerous references are made to lost books, which would be invaluable prizes if they could be recovered now, though it is unlikely that they ever will be, "The Book of the Acts of Solomon," "The Chronicles of the Kings of Judah," and "The Chronicles of the Kings of Israel."

These references are not to the books of I and II Chronicles as we have them in the Bible. Our two books of Chronicles were written much later, after the return from exile, and retell many of the events recorded in the books of Samuel and Kings, from a priestly slant, with long lists of genealogy and much moralizing. They are less authentic history. The author dwells at length on the blessings that come to those who keep the law of Yahweh and the punishments that befall transgressors, and apparently does not hesitate to exaggerate these blessings and calamities to prove his point. It is a principle of historical interpretation which we find repeatedly illustrated, that the more nearly contemporary a piece of writing, the more direct, natural, and authentic the account.

Storytellers and Editors

But we are getting ahead of the story. We must go back now to the ninth century, approximately to 850 B.C., in the period of the divided kingdom. At this time some extremely important writing took place without which we should be missing a great deal in the Old Testament.

About 850 B.C. some writer in the Southern Kingdom with a marvelous storytelling gift either wrote out for the first time, or compiled with such changes as his own personality prompted, a series of stories relating the early history of his people. These tales had been preserved by the women as they gathered with their water bottles at the wells, by the men as they chatted around the campfires and as they told the stories of the great past to their young sons. A great deal of the early Old Testament had long been in the making before any of it got written down. Just how much of it was passed along solely by word of mouth, and how much had been written down in fragments before any of it was put together consecutively, we have no sure way of knowing.

Beginning with the second chapter of Genesis, these stories appear along with other material throughout the Pentateuch, Joshua, Judges, and into the books of Samuel. They are vivid, dramatic, and full of conversation and human interest. Here we find not only our earliest creation story (that of the first chapter of Genesis, as we shall note presently, came much later) and the expulsion of Adam and Eve from Eden for their disobedience, but also the doings of the patriarchs—Abraham, Isaac and Jacob, Joseph in Egypt, Moses leading his people through the desert, Joshua leading them in their rugged attempts to gain a foothold in Canaan. To get a sampling of these tales, one would do well to read the stories of Adam and Eve and their sons Cain and Abel in Genesis 2:4—4:15, or the doom of Sodom in Genesis 18, or the betrothal of Isaac and Rebekah in Genesis 24, or the decline and fall of Samson in Judges 16, or the story of David and Goliath in I Samuel 17.

The stories from the hand of this great ninth century writer are rapidly-moving narrative, but they are more. They are a testimony to God's leading and care and his demand for righteousness, and to Israel's sense of being a divinely chosen people with a great destiny if they would be faithful. Seldom if ever has narrative been used as skillfully to teach a religious lesson.

Who was this nameless storyteller? Bible scholars have given him a name, and we call him "J." There is a double reason for this. The predominant setting of the stories in the south, together with linguistic peculiarities which only a Hebrew scholar would detect, indicates that the writing was done by somebody in the kingdom of Judah. Furthermore, the writer's name for God is *YHWH,* translated "Jehovah" in the American Standard Version, although *Yahweh* is nearer the original. In the Moffatt translation, the "J" passages are printed in italics through Genesis and Exodus, and it is interesting to read these passages, skipping the rest, and note their characteristics.

But what comes between these "J" stories? "J" was not the only great storyteller of the Hebrews, for somewhat later, probably about 750 B.C., another skilled narrator appeared who was partial to the northern heroes. Because he wrote from the standpoint of the tribe of Ephraim and used the generic term *El* or *Elohim* for God, we call him "E." The ethical sense of the "E" writer, or writers, seems more developed; the conception of God is more spiritual and less anthropomorphic. The "E" stories are not usually so forceful as the "J," but they have a smoother literary style. To sample them, read the story of the attempted sacrifice of Isaac in Genesis 22:1-14, Jacob's flight from Laban in Genesis 31, the finding of the baby Moses in Exodus 1:15— 2:10, Aaron and the golden calf in Exodus 32:1-6, 15-24, Joshua's farewell address in Joshua 24:14-25, Jotham's fable in Judges 9:6-21, or the boy Samuel in I Samuel 1 and 3. One may detect them in the Moffatt translation by the fact that they are enclosed in square brackets.

How did the "J" and "E" manuscripts become merged? After the Northern Kingdom fell with the capture of Samaria by the Assyrians in 722 B.C., the literary treasures of the north passed into southern hands. Sometime between that date and the fall of Jerusalem in 586 B.C., some editor or editors wove "J" and "E" together to form a consecutive narrative. A reading in the Moffatt translation of the Joseph cycle, found in Genesis 37 through 48, will give a clear idea of how these two strands are interwoven. We do not know who did it or why, but since the prophets were suppressed under King Manasseh, it may be that somebody who could not speak openly wanted to remind the people of their great obligations and high destiny by a composite version of God's dealings with their fathers.

But the interweaving is not ended yet. Both "J" and "E" were storytellers, interested aplenty in morals as they understood them, but not mainly in the legal aspects of morality. In the year 621 B.C., King Josiah ordered that the Temple in Jerusalem be repaired, and in the process a certain "book of the law" was found. This important document became the basis of a great reform in which the heathen shrines were cast down and the king and the people together took a solemn vow to live by its provisions, many of which were in keeping with the ethical teachings of the prophets. How did it get there? It may have been written as early as 650 B.C. and accidently discovered; quite likely it was "planted" there to be discovered. In any case this code, which we call "D," became the main structure of our Book of Deuteronomy. Then later, during the Babylonian captivity, some devout Jew or Jews amalgamated "D" with the already existing "JE."

This "D" code is the first example of canonized Scripture, for when it was found in the Temple it made such an impression on the king that he sent to "inquire of Yahweh" about it by way of the prophetess Huldah, who endorsed it as being truly the word of the Lord. However, it is not the first law code, for there is an earlier one in Exodus 20:22—23:33. Deuteronomy gets its name from the assumption that as "the second law," it recapitulates all that had preceded it.

Up to this point we have "JED." But the story of the making of the early Old Testament has still another chapter. After the return from exile, the priests who were then directing Israel's religious affairs took their turn at writing history. What they were most concerned to do was to show how the sacred ritualistic observances had come into being, and hence their divine authority. So they divided history into epochs: from the creation to the flood, with the sabbath as the climax of creation;[5] from the flood to the time of Abram, with the prohibition against eating blood introduced after the flood;[6] from Abram to Moses, with circumcision beginning in the time of Abram;[7] and from Moses onward, in whose time the Passover was introduced.[8] A third

---

[5] Gen. 2:2-4   [7] Gen. 17:9-27
[6] Gen. 9:4   [8] Exod. 12:1-14

law code was incorporated, the Holiness Code,[9] which is so called because it mainly stresses ritualistic and ceremonial purity though it does contain the great commandment, "Love thy neighbor as thyself."[10] Much of the "P" document, as this work of the priestly writers is called, is from our standpoint quite uninspiring, with long genealogies as well as outmoded laws, but we must ever be grateful for its great hymn of creation with which the Bible opens.[11]

Although "P" originated about 500 B.C., the composing and editing of it went on for a century. During this time it was amalgamated with the already existing "JED" to form "JEDP." So, by approximately the beginning of the fourth century B.C., the first five books of the Bible, which the Jews call the Torah, were substantially as they stand today.

It is apparent even from this brief summary that the old idea that Moses wrote the Pentateuch (including even the account of his own death!) has to be abandoned. The original formulation of the Ten Commandments under God's leading may indeed have come from his hand. But the greater part of the Pentateuch in its elements, and all of it in its present form, is later. In view of how it grew by stages, it is not surprising that it contains fascinating folklore and a primitive, though dramatic and spiritually meaningful, explanation of the creation, the coming of sin into the world, and the emergence of toil and pain and strife. Furthermore, in history that in its outlines is authentic though not in every detail, it gives the record of how God mercifully led his chosen but erring people in the way of righteousness.

---

[9] Lev. 17—26   [10] Lev. 19:18   [11] Gen. 1:1—2:4

LATER HISTORY

We have now traced the emergence of the most important historical writings of the Old Testament, but we have not quite finished. Reference has been made to the postexilic writing of pre-exilic history as found in I and II Chronicles. The books of Ezra and Nehemiah were probably written by the author of Chronicles, often referred to for lack of a more definite name as "the Chronicler." He doubtless had access to the memoirs of Nehemiah,[12] an exceedingly able and vigorous young governor who took charge of the rebuilding of Jerusalem after it had lain in ruins a century and half, and he may also have had those of Ezra the priest and scribe. While these books are not as great history or literature as the David stories or the writings of "J" and "E," they are our chief source of information as to what happened between the return from exile in 538 B.C. and the rise of the Maccabees in 168 B.C. In general these books reflect the legalistic and ritualistic emphases current in that day.

If one wishes to read in more detail the interweaving of these various strands to form the historical books of the Old Testament, it is to be found in many books of which Professor Julius Bewer's *An Introduction to the Literature of the Old Testament* and Elmer W. K. Mould's *Essentials of Bible History* are among the best. But even this short survey must have made clear some points. First, that the Bible was not written in the order in which we have it arranged. Second, that much human frailty as well as human genius went into its making, with some of the most skilled writers of all time, yet men like

---

[12] See Neh. 2:9-16; also chapters 4 and 6. The story of Nehemiah's secret survey of the city by night and its hazardous rebuilding are especially vivid passages.

ourselves, among its creators. Third, that God was moving in these writers and in the experience of the people in a marvelous way. The fact that the Old Testament has a composite authorship, with legend mixed in with fact and much of the history written from a religious bias, ought not to overshadow the greater fact that through it God speaks. Were it not in a true sense inspired, it would not through the ages have been inspiring many millions to better living and to a higher discernment of the Eternal.

Hebrew Prophecy

We must now look at another large segment of the Old Testament, the writings of the prophets. A prophet is not primarily a foreteller of events, though the Hebrew prophets often had keen discernment as to the signs of the times; rather, he is a forthteller, a spokesman for the Lord. The Old Testament prophets had a message and produced a literature which for religious passion and ethical discernment has not been equaled anywhere outside the words of Jesus.

EARLY PROPHETS

Not all the prophets wrote. Moses and Samuel were prophets as well as statesmen. Nathan in the Parable of the One Ewe Lamb adroitly charged the great King David with sin,[13] and later, the prophet Elijah boldly confronted King Ahab and charged him with murder in the affair of Naboth's vineyard.[14] Elijah and, still more his successor, Elisha, were involved in the revolution that led to the fall of the house of Omri to which

---

[13] II Sam. 12:1-15   [14] I Kings 21

Ahab belonged. But none of these, though they are vividly written about, wrote their own messages. They are therefore sometimes called the preliterary prophets.

SEVEN GREAT PROPHETS

Amos.—The prophet who gave us the earliest complete book in the Bible is Amos. He lived about 750 B.C., approximately a century later than Elijah and Elisha. A humble herdsman of Tekoa, he appeared one day at the royal shrine of Bethel and, with a religious earnestness that moves us even yet as we read it, began to denounce the spiritual shallowness, the exploitation of the poor by the rich, the bribery, sexual indulgence, and general moral laxity which he saw all about him. With consummate skill Amos won his audience by denouncing the sins of Israel's neighbors and then struck home to their own transgressions in the eyes of God.

> Thus saith the Lord: For three transgressions of Israel, and for four, I will not turn away the punishment thereof; . . . You only have I known of all the families of the earth: therefore I will punish you for all your iniquities.[15]

But the message is not all invective, for we find him also saying,

> Seek Jehovah, and ye shall live; . . . let justice roll down as waters, and righteousness as a mighty stream.[16]

Hosea.—Soon after, perhaps a decade later, came Hosea, a sensitive, tender soul who stressed the forgiving mercy of God, as Amos had the divine justice. Out of personal suffering he had come to know God's love, for his own wife had drifted

---

[15] Amos 2:6; 3:2   [16] Amos 5:6, 24, A.S.V.

into infidelity and when he was tempted to let her go his love led him to forgive her and bring her back to his home. How much more must God love his sinful people! One of the most beautiful passages in the Bible is that in which Hosea has God say,

> When Israel was a child, then I loved him, and called my son out of Egypt. . . . I taught Ephraim to walk; I took them on my arms; but they knew not that I healed them.[17]

Isaiah.—About the time Hosea was prophesying in the north, a young man appeared in the south who was destined to be a very great prophet and statesman. The work of Isaiah spans the forty-year period from about 740 B.C. through 701, when Jerusalem was besieged by King Sennacherib of Assyria and narrowly escaped destruction. Not all of the book which bears his name was written by him, but most of the first thirty-nine chapters were. In his matchless sixth chapter Isaiah tells us that "in the year that king Uzziah died" he had a vision as he was praying in the temple which led him to feel God was calling him to preach to his sinful, dull-spirited countrymen, and he responded, "Here am I; send me." The rest of his life was spent in speaking for God with courage and clear discernment.

One finds in Isaiah's messages a union of those of Amos and Hosea, for he stressed both the justice and the mercy of God. He has a particularly vivid invective against the idle, luxury-loving women of the time.[18] There is great moral vigor in his words:

---

[17] Hos. 11:1, 3, 4, A.S.V.   [18] Isa. 3:16—4:1

> Wash you, make you clean; . . . cease to do evil; learn
> to do well; seek justice, relieve the oppressed, judge the
> fatherless, plead for the widow,[19]

and there is equally great promise in

> Though your sins be as scarlet, they shall be as white
> as snow. . . .[20]

Isaiah was a highly original prophet. Politically, he steadily
though not always successfully advised the kings to trust in
God and avoid entangling alliances. One of his greatest ad-
monitions,

> In returning and rest shall ye be saved; in quietness
> and in confidence shall be your strength,[21]

probably had originally a national significance which we would
do well to recapture. Religiously, he had an enlarged conception of God, seeing Assyria as well as Israel under Yahweh's
control and the nation's enemies as the rod of God's anger
upon his sinful people. But we find also in Isaiah's writings
the beginnings of the messianic hope that "a remnant shall
return"[22] and a deliverer be raised up by God to establish the
ideal kingdom of the future. One aspect of this messianic hope
was the prophecy of a warless world when men should "beat
their swords into plowshares, and their spears into pruninghooks"[23]; another the coming of a child whose "name shall be
called Wonderful, Counsellor, The mighty God, The everlasting Father, The Prince of Peace,"[24] to rule upon the throne
of David with justice and righteousness forever.

---

[19] Isa. 1:16, 17, A.S.V.
[20] Isa. 1:18
[21] Isa. 30:15
[22] Isa. 10:21, A.S.V.
[23] Isa. 2:4
[24] Isa. 9:6,7

Micah.—Contemporary with the latter part of Isaiah's ministry was the work of Micah, who was greatly troubled at the way the poor people in the country had to suffer from the attacks the nation's leaders had stupidly precipitated, while the rich could live in relative safety behind the walls of Jerusalem. Micah in a single immortal sentence summed up the meaning of religion:

He hath showed thee, O man, what is good; and what doth the Lord require of thee, but to do justly, and to love mercy, and to walk humbly with thy God?[25]

Jeremiah.—Jeremiah is one of the greatest figures of all time. We know more about him than we do about most of the prophets, for he had a secretary, Baruch, who preserved not only his thoughts but also many incidents from his life. We know that he felt he was called of God from before his birth and that he had "a burning fire shut up in [his] bones" [26] that would not let him rest until he spoke the truth as he saw it. Because his message was unpopular, he was put in the stocks, thrown into a miry cistern, imprisoned, had his writings burned, and in general was persecuted by the king, the people, and the false prophets who said what the rulers wanted to hear. What got Jeremiah into such disfavor was not only his invectives against the prevalent sin and profligacy, but also his repeated warnings that it was folly to resist the conquerors from the east since Jerusalem was bound to fall. Fall it did, after much destruction which could have been avoided had his advice been heeded. When the leaders were carried away

[25] Mic. 6:8   [26] Jer. 20:9

to Babylon in 597 B.C. and again in 586 B.C., Jeremiah was left behind, but he was later dragged along to Egypt by the survivors who fled in that direction, and there he probably died a martyr.

Jeremiah lives in history while those who called him a traitor have long since been forgotten. But it is not simply as a courageous figure daring to speak his mind that he holds so high a place. He had a deep, strong faith in God. Realistic as he was about Jerusalem's immediate fate, he nevertheless foresaw a glorious day when God would make a new covenant which would be written in men's hearts. There is little if any-thing else in the Old Testament which comes so close to the spirit of the New as these words he represents Yahweh as speaking:

> Yea, I have loved thee with an everlasting love: therefore with lovingkindness have I drawn thee. . . .
> But this is the covenant that I will make with the house of Israel after those days, saith Jehovah: I will put my law in their inward parts, and in their heart will I write it; and I will be their God, and they shall be my people. . . . I will forgive their iniquity, and their sin will I remember no more.[27]

Ezekiel.—Toward the end of Jeremiah's ministry in Jerusalem another prophet arose in Babylon—of lesser stature but still a man of great spiritual insight. He was among those deported in the exile. We shall linger with Ezekiel only long enough to point out that among the cryptic visions with which his book abounds there is a steady emphasis on the majesty, the holiness, and the omnipresence of God. His allegory of

---

[27] Jer. 31:3, 33, 34, A.S.V.

the eagles and the vine in the seventeenth chapter not only introduces a new literary type but also implies Isaiah's doctrine of the remnant. Chapter eighteen is a fine essay on individual, as contrasted with inherited, responsibility, and the thirty-fourth chapter is a beautiful portrait of God as the shepherd of his people.

Second Isaiah.—One more great prophet we must speak of, perhaps the greatest of them all. We do not even know his name, but we call him the Second Isaiah or Deutero-Isaiah because his message is found in the latter part of the Book of Isaiah, beginning at chapter forty. These chapters reveal a background so very different from the first part of the book that they could not have been written by the eighth century Isaiah. The Exile had already taken place, but whether the second Isaiah wrote around 540 B.C., as some scholars think from references to the Persian king Cyrus, or a century later, is not certain.

The second Isaiah was a poet of a high order, and some of the most moving lyrics of the Bible are from his pen. It is not by accident that much of the text of Handel's *Messiah* is taken from his words. And he could not have been so great a poet had he not had a great deal to say.

Foremost among his ideas is a clear-cut monotheism. Early Hebrew thought, you will recall, was not monotheistic but henotheistic, the belief in the existence of many gods but the supremacy of one. "Thou shalt have no other gods before me," reflects this framework. Israel's religious leaders had been moving towards monotheism, and the prophetic idea that Yahweh was using Israel's enemies as his agents in bringing judgment on his sinful people was a long step towards recognition of his universal sway. Yet it remained for the second Isaiah to represent Yahweh as saying unequivocally,

> I am the first, and I am the last; and beside me there is no God. . . . I form the light, and create darkness; I make peace, and create evil; I the Lord do all these things.[28]

But Yahweh's universal control is not in power only, but in redeeming love also. His purpose includes the salvation of the Gentiles as well as the Jews, and he is as near to those in exile as to those in Jerusalem. Furthermore, their exile and sufferings have come not solely as punishment for sin, though they are that; they have befallen the Jews to purify them to act as God's servants in carrying the message of redemption to all the world. To be God's chosen people means not that they are chosen for favors, but for service! This twofold idea of vicarious and redemptive suffering and of God's universal love for all men comes to its highest expression in the fifty-third chapter of Isaiah. This "suffering servant" chapter was probably written to set forth God's mission for Israel, but because it describes so exactly the perfect Suffering Servant, it was long thought to be a direct prevision of Christ.

Like the first Isaiah and Jeremiah, Deutero-Isaiah foresaw the coming of a messiah who should redeem Israel and usher in a new age. Among his most vivid pictures are those of a highway through the desert, a way of righteousness leading from sin and affliction to a new heaven and a new earth where the glory of the Lord would be revealed and men would live in peace and happiness. The only way to catch the full majesty

---

[28] Isa. 44:6; 45:7.

of such passages is to read some of them; as, for example, chapters 40, 42:1-9, 51, 55, 60, 61, 65:17-25.

LATER PROPHETS

We must not stop longer with the other prophets, though others there were. Neither their dates nor sequence is certain, but it is probable that Zephaniah, Nahum, and Habakkuk, as well as Jeremiah, lived in the seventh century and that the writings of Haggai, Zechariah, Obadiah, and Malachi are to be located in the sixth and fifth centuries. Joel, written around 400 B.C., is the last of the prophetic books. By this time the light of prophecy was spent. None of these prophets was as original or as great in religious insights as the seven we have examined, and some of them, notably Nahum, fiercely pronounce judgment on Israel's foes in a way far removed from the tender love of God as we find it in Hosea and the Second Isaiah. This is another reminder that we cannot possibly read the Bible and get its message straight if we assume that it is all on one level of inspiration.

Hebrew Poetry

We have had occasion to refer to the poetry of the Old Testament, for it appears mixed in with the history, and many of the most vivid prophetic utterances are poems. We must now look at it a little more closely.

The distinguishing mark of Hebrew poetry is not rhyme or meter, though it has a kind of rhythm. Rather, it is *parallelism,* a symmetrical arrangement of ideas. There is *synonymous* parallelism, in which the second line repeats the first in slightly different form.

The law of the Lord is perfect, restoring the soul:
The testimony of the Lord is sure, making wise the
    simple.[29]

There is *synthetic* parallelism, where the second line builds up
from the first.

I will sing unto the Lord, for he hath triumphed glo-
    riously;
The horse and his rider hath he thrown into the sea.[30]

There is *antithetic* parallelism, where the second line gives a
contrast to the first.

A soft answer turneth away wrath;
But a grievous word stirreth up anger.[31]

There is also the more complex *stairlike* parallelism in which
each line in a series amplifies the preceding.

For, lo, the winter is past;
The rain is over and gone;
The flowers appear on the earth;
The time of the singing of birds is come,
And the voice of the turtle-dove is heard in our land.[32]

The foregoing examples illustrate also the principal types
of biblical poetry from the standpoint of theme and subject
matter. The greater part of it is religious in nature, as we
have it in the devotional poetry of the Psalms and the im-
passioned words of the prophets. The Psalms were not all
written by David, as formerly supposed, though he may have
written some of them. The Book of Psalms is the hymnbook
of the second Temple, erected after the return from exile, and

---

[29] Ps. 19:7, A.S.V.
[30] Exod. 15:1.
[31] Prov. 15:1, A.S.V.
[32] Song of Sol. 2:11, 12, A.S.V.

in it we have a compilation of great hymns through which the people voiced their aspirations, their thanksgivings, their plaints, their trust in Yahweh in the midst of both joy and adversity.

There is also much national and patriotic poetry in the Old Testament, most of it early folksongs that got woven into the "JEDP" story. Among these are the "Song of Miriam" in Exodus 15, the "Song of Deborah" in Judges 5, the "Blessing of Isaac" in Genesis 27:27-29, the "Blessing of Jacob" in Genesis 49, and the "Blessing of Moses" in Deuteronomy 33. This does not mean that all these persons were poets. No one knows who composed these songs, but the people sang them with patriotic fervor in much the same mood that now prompts Americans to sing "The Star-Spangled Banner."

A third type of poetry is didactic and philosophical. The Book of Proverbs, abounding in antithetical parallelism, is just what the name suggests—a collection of pungent adages. A greater piece of wisdom poetry is the philosophic drama of Job, of which we must say another word presently.

A fourth type is the lyrics of romantic love. This is what we have, bordering on the erotic, in the Song of Solomon. When it was formerly thought that this in some way foreshadowed the marriage of Christ and his Church, its meaning was completely obscured. It is not great poetry or great religion, but it shows us that the Hebrews were many-sided in their interests! Some of the mystics, particularly Bernard of Clairvaux and St. John of the Cross, have based much of their spiritual writing on it.

A fifth kind of poetry is the dirge. This appears with great poignancy in the Book of Lamentations. This is also a form of national poetry, for its theme is the sufferings of those who were left in Jerusalem after its fall.

Hebrew Philosophy

We referred a moment ago to the wisdom literature. This includes the books of Proverbs, Job, and Ecclesiastes, all of which were probably put together in the fourth and third centuries B.C. Some of the Psalms are also of this nature.

The Book of Proverbs is an assemblage of collections of adages, probably at least five of them of varying dates. It abounds in "quotable quotes," with many a sly dig at such human frailties as laziness, gossip and argumentativeness, and not a little humor. Among its most beautiful passages are those in praise of wisdom in chapters 3, 4, and 8, and its graphic picture of a model wife in 31:10-31.

The Book of Job is one of the greatest pieces of literature ever written. It deals with the perennial problem of human suffering—not the suffering for sin which the prophets had many times talked of, but the suffering of the righteous. It was ordinarily believed by the Hebrews not only that righteousness brought reward and sin brought suffering, but also that *all* suffering was somehow traceable to sin. The unknown author of this book had the temerity to challenge this assumption in a drama in which God agreed to let Satan test the loyalty of Job, a righteous man, by stripping him of his possessions, his children, and his health. It consists mainly of cycles of dialogue between Job and his conventionally-minded friends, but comes to a grand climax when God speaks to him out of the whirlwind. What the Voice says gives no solution.

but something better—a sense of mastery through the power of the Eternal. Some later hand missed the whole point of the book and added an epilogue in which Job got back everything he had lost, but the curtain really falls at the point where he is able to say to Yahweh:

> I had heard of thee by the hearing of the ear;
> But now mine eye seeth thee.[33]

The Book of Ecclesiastes is in a very different vein. Its unknown author, who calls himself Koheleth (a "gatherer of an assembly," though most versions translate it "preacher"), had apparently come in touch with Greek Epicurean philosophy, and what he has given us is a blend of Hebrew and Greek worldly wisdom. Its main theme is the emptiness and futility of existence, but it contains nevertheless some fine passages. Among these are his affirmation, in the third chapter, of a God-given time for everything, and his exquisitely beautiful description of old age in the last chapter.

Short Stories

Have we finished? No, not quite. To one accustomed to thinking of the Bible as historical throughout, it may be a surprise to discover that it contains also short stories—some of the finest fiction ever written. (Fiction, we must remember, is not the same as falsehood; at its best it consists of imaginative stories through which truth is imparted, as Jesus used parables in the New Testament.) A story does not have to be literal historical fact to contain a great and permanent meaning.

---

[33] Job 42:5, A.S.V.

The loveliest of all these stories is the Book of Ruth. Though placed in our Bible between Judges and I Kings because its historical setting is in the period of the "judges," it was probably written in the third century B.C. as an answer to the racial exclusiveness that had become acutely prevalent. Nehemiah had forbidden the intermarriage of Jews with persons of any other race. But here was a reminder that David, their greatest king, had a beautiful-spirited Moabitess for his great-grandmother!

The Book of Jonah is another little book with a great message—the missionary message of the love of God for the people of Nineveh as well as for those of Jerusalem. In story form, the contrast between the churlishness of the self-righteous Jonah and the universal love of God, which the second Isaiah had taught, becomes strikingly clear. Its theme is aptly expressed in our hymn,

> There's a wideness in God's mercy
> Like the wideness of the sea.[34]

One of the worst mistakes ever made about the Bible was the missing of this great message in futile argument over the dimensions of the whale's gullet.

A graphic story with a less beautiful theme is the Book of Esther. Its overtones are those of Jewish pride and a spirit of revenge resulting from the persecutions the Jews had had to undergo. It is apparently designed to give historical justification for the observance of the feast of Purim, which the Jews may have taken over from the Persians during their captivity. Despite the fact that it does not have a very great

[34] By Frederick Faber.

theme, Mordecai's challenge to Queen Esther, "And who knows whether you have not come to the kingdom for such a time as this?"[35] is still a challenge to us today.

We have now said something about the origins of every book in the Old Testament except Daniel. This was the last to be written, and we can date it with more accuracy than most because it was almost certainly written between 168 and 165 B.C. During this period the Jews revolted against their despotic Syrian overlord Antiochus Epiphanes, and someone who was unable to speak openly, but who wanted to rally the Jews to trust God in remembrance of their past and to predict the doom of their conquerors, wrote this book. It is a combination of historical story, with the scene laid in the time of King Nebuchadnezzar, and a new type of writing, the apocalyptic literature. This latter type, expressing ideas through cryptic symbolism cast in the form of visions, was common in the period between the Testaments and we shall meet it again in the Book of Revelation. The story part of Daniel in the first six chapters is a vivid call to go through the fiery furnace or the lions' den of persecution, sustained by the sure presence of God.

This survey has given a few signposts along the way to an understanding of a marvelous collection of great books. But signposts, without a personal journey, will not carry one to a destination. If one wants to see for himself how truly great the Old Testament is, he should read in their context at least the passages to which references have been made. And when this has been done, one will want to read more.

---

[35] Esther 4:14, R.S.V.

CHAPTER FOUR

How the New Testament Was Written

In reviewing the steps by which the Old Testament came into being, we dealt with each main type of literature separately and for the most part traced in chronological sequence the appearance of the books, one by one. There it was natural to begin with the history, for while some very early folksongs antedate any written history and the prophecy of Amos was the earliest complete book, an important part of the history found in the Old Testament was written before any other major type of literature emerged. This was not the case in the New Testament.

The historical events around which the New Testament is centered are indeed primary. Christianity is, through and through, a historical religion, and except for the coming of Jesus Christ into the world, his life, his teachings, his death and resurrection, and the establishment of the Church as the community of his followers, we should have neither Christianity nor New Testament. But this does not mean that the writing of the record of these events came first. The events took place; the Church was founded; and out of the experience and needs of the Christians of the first and early second centuries the writings came. We are apt to assume that the New

Testament produced the Church, but the contrary is the case —the Church gave rise to the New Testament.

The New Testament was not written to create a sacred literature. Although the early Christian writers had the Old Testament as their Scriptures, not one of them had any idea that he was writing something that would itself become Holy Writ. Nevertheless God used them, as he had used the Old Testament storytellers, prophets, poets, and seers, to write eternal truth that still inspires and quickens our spirits. The New Testament, written by human authors, is not flawless; yet it stands pre-eminent among all the books ever written. To doubt its inspiration would be folly; on the other hand, to take it as literally inspired and therefore all of one level would be to miss the great events and the lights and shadows of experience that brought it into being.

The New Testament is obviously shorter than the Old. It contains only twenty-seven books instead of thirty-nine, but it is even shorter than this would indicate because there is no long book in it and some of the letters are very brief. It is also in simpler form, for it contains only three main literary types: letter, historical record, and apocalypse, all interspersed with spiritual and moral wisdom. The marvel is that this one small book—a collection of still smaller books—survived the fires of persecution and the changing patterns of culture to remain, after nineteen centuries, the world's most significant literature and greatest spiritual treasure-house.

Our procedure will be to (1) trace rapidly the familiar but eternally important events that brought both Christianity and the New Testament into being, (2) examine Paul's letters, (3) see how the Gospels and the Book of Acts came into being, (4) look at the books emerging from persecution— Hebrews, I Peter, and the Book of Revelation, and (5) take a concluding look at the other letters. Though there is some disagreement among scholars, this outline follows in general the order in which the books were written.

THE GOSPEL STORY

Fulton Oursler has called it "The Greatest Story Ever Told" —this story of the coming of Jesus to live among men the life of God, to save men from their sins and inner defeat, and to impart new life through faith. So it is, and the story is not ended, for Jesus Christ is still doing it. The New Testament is concerned with that part of this endless story which deals with the earthly life of Jesus and the coming of his Spirit to establish the Christian community and send his followers out as flaming witnesses of their faith.

The story does not begin with the birth of Jesus in the Bethlehem stable nor with his conception in the womb of Mary nine months earlier. It begins back in the Old Testament in God's covenant with his people, in their quest for him, in their apostasies and God's righteous judgments, in the collapse of their national security, in God's promise that a remnant of the faithful will survive and that to them a Deliverer will come. Most of the Jews were looking for a messiah who would restore their national greatness and sit again on the throne of David; others were looking for a messiah, as described in Daniel and in the apocalyptic books written between the Testaments, who would descend from heaven with great glory to judge the earth. What they were not looking for was a savior who would be born as a baby in a manger, grow up in a poor man's home, become a wandering preacher, and finally die on a cross like any common felon. But the ways of God are wiser than the expectations of men.

Jesus was born while Herod the Great was king, and since Herod died in 4 B.C., he was probably born between 6 and 4 B.C. No one knows what day of the year, but ever since the fourth century December 25, celebrated in the Mithra cult as the winter solstice and the sun's birthday, has been observed by the Christian Church. We are told nothing of Jesus' childhood or youth except for the one vivid incident of his visit to the Temple in Jerusalem at the age of twelve. But since Mary and Joseph were devout Jews, and Jesus quotes so often from the Old Testament, we can surmise that he grew up an eager, thoughtful boy, saturated in the wisdom of the Jewish Scriptures. He had four brothers and two sisters, and after Joseph's death was doubtless the chief breadwinner. The story of these hidden years, if we could recover it, would be of incalculable interest. It was not preserved because the Gospel writers were gripped only by the amazing events of Jesus' ministry, death, and resurrection appearances, and had none of our concern for general biographical portraiture or the psychological analysis of personalities.

Jesus' public ministry lasted at most three years, possibly not more than one. He wrote nothing. He died a young man. Into the brief period of which we have a record are compressed his baptism by John the Baptist—a prophet of the Old Testament stamp—his time of solitary meditation and temptation in the wilderness, the calling of his twelve most intimate disciples, his going about with them healing and teaching in Galilee and its environs, the journey to Jerusalem and his triumphal entry, the stormy events of passion week, his crucifixion, and resurrection. The surprising thing is not that there are some discrepancies in the accounts, but that we have so nearly convergent and clear a picture as we have. We can doubt this incident or that in the record, for as we shall note presently there was no contemporary written report. But we cannot doubt that Jesus lived, and was the God-centered, loving, serving, forgiving, healing, outwardly-defeated but spiritually-triumphant person that the Gospels bring vividly before us.

Somewhere along the way—we cannot be sure just when— Jesus apparently became convinced that he was the promised Messiah. But of quite a different kind from what the Jews were looking for! He had no political aspirations, and while he appears to have shared the common expectation of a coming apocalyptic intervention, he conceived his own mission as one of humble, loving service to all men at the call of God. In faith and love he called men to faith and love, teaching the conditions of entrance into the Kingdom by simple but vivid parables and healing the souls and bodies of people wherever he went. There is little, if anything, in his teaching not found somewhere in the Old Testament, but the unerring insight by which he picked out the important things and the fidelity with which he lived what he taught made people see in him something altogether new. "The common people heard him gladly," but the high priests and rulers were alarmed for fear that their own status was jeopardized, the people were fickle, and together they brought him to his death.

Although we have Peter's great affirmation at Caesarea Philippi, "Thou art the Christ, the Son of the living God,"[1]

---

[1] Matt. 16:16

there is little evidence that before his death the people in general regarded him as the Messiah. Probably his closest disciples, like the people who waved palm branches and cried, "Hosanna to the son of David," as he entered Jerusalem,[2] did not really grasp this great fact. But, when on the first Easter morning and thereafter he began to appear to them, individually and in groups, as a living Presence, those closest to him were convinced of it. Discouragement then gave way to joyous fervor.

The little company of the Twelve, in this resurrection faith, grew to one hundred and twenty, and after Peter's great sermon on Pentecost three thousand more were added to the fellowship. Aflame with a faith to which they felt they must bear witness at all costs, these early Christians braved the fires of public derision and persecution. Among them were valiant souls who at great risk and hardship went here, there, and everywhere, preaching the gospel. The greatest of them was Paul, radically converted from a life of persecuting the Christians to be the first great evangelist, missionary, theologian, and administrator of the Christian Church. The story of these missionary journeys is a major portion of the Book of Acts We glean many incidents also from Paul's letters to the churches that were founded throughout Asia Minor, in Macedonia, and Greece, and as far west as Rome. These letters were the first written documents of the New Testament.

THE LETTERS OF PAUL

These letters, like all of the New Testament, were written in the Greek vernacular used throughout that part of the world.[3]

---

[2] Matt. 21:9   [3] Jesus and his disciples spoke Aramaic.

Paul was following a common practice of the time in writing letters. They were carried by individuals as they went from city to city. Travel, though slow and primitive compared with the present, was facilitated by the extensive system of Roman roads. Paul's letters all follow a general pattern: they begin with a salutation and affectionate greeting to the persons addressed, state the message, and end with a benediction. Some were signed with a brief note in his own handwriting,[4] but in general he appears to have dictated them. There are nine, possibly ten, of these letters to the churches (Ephesians being of disputed authorship) ; and three others, I and II Timothy and Titus, called the Pastoral Epistles, may have been written by Paul but more likely were the work of some unknown Christian toward the close of the first century or even later.

The writing of the letters that we know were Paul's began about the year 50, during his second missionary journey. Bible scholars disagree as to whether I Thessalonians or Galatians is earlier. Following the usual view, we shall discuss the Thessalonian letters first.

I and II Thessalonians.—If you will follow Paul's journey in Acts 15:22—18:22, tracing it on the map, you will note that he went north from Jerusalem to Antioch; then northwest through Asia Minor to Troas (the Troy of the *Iliad,* the *Odyssey,* and the *Aeneid*) ; across into Macedonia, where he founded a church at Thessalonica; south to Athens; and then a short distance west to Corinth. It was while he was staying there that Silas and Timothy arrived from Macedonia and brought such news from the Thessalonian church that Paul felt

---

[4] See endings of I Cor., Col., II Thess.

impelled to write this church two letters. It was probably also at Corinth that disquieting news about the Judaizers in the Galatian churches reached him and prompted him to write a letter to this community.

Things may not have been going very smoothly at the Thessalonian church, for there was a riot at the time of its establishment (Acts 17:1-10), and persecution later (I Thess. 2:13-16). Paul writes to reassure them regarding his leadership and to commend their steadfastness, but most of all to answer a question that had been bothering many. Nearly all the Christians of that time, Paul included, were looking for a speedy second coming of Christ, and the Thessalonians were worried about what would happen to their loved ones who might die before it happened. Although he wisely assured them that God would take care of "those who have fallen asleep," his own picture of the second coming as it appears in both letters shows that his thought regarding it had not progressed much beyond current Jewish apocalyptic ideas. We can reject this and still find great truth and power in such injunctions as,

> Rejoice always; pray without ceasing; in everything give thanks: for this is the will of God in Christ Jesus. . . . [5]

Galatians.—Galatia is a province near the middle of Asia Minor. Paul had founded some churches there on his first missionary journey and he revisited them on the second. A great controversy had arisen as to whether, in order to become a Christian, a Gentile must submit to the Jewish rite of cir-

---

[5] I Thess. 5:16-18, A.S.V.

cumcision. Both Peter and Paul said No—a very important decision since otherwise Christianity would have become a Jewish sect. Some who are called Judaizers thought otherwise, and though the matter was apparently settled at Jerusalem (Acts 15), some Judaizers went up to Galatia and made trouble there. The Epistle to the Galatians is a great declaration of Christian liberty. The first two chapters give important biographical data about Paul, and the second makes his position crystal clear. It is summed up in, "A man is not justified by the works of the law but through faith in Jesus Christ."[6] The letter contains some of Paul's greatest words of spiritual insight, such as:

> I have been crucified with Christ, and it is no longer I that live, but Christ liveth in me.[7]
>
> There is neither Jew nor Greek, there is neither slave nor free, there is neither male nor female; for you are all one in Christ Jesus.[8]
>
> The fruit of the Spirit is love, joy, peace, longsuffering, kindness, goodness, faithfulness, meekness, self-control; against such there is no law.[9]

I and II Corinthians.—The next letters of Paul that were preserved (for doubtless a number of others after being read were destroyed) are I and II Corinthians. These were written during a three-year stay at Ephesus on his third missionary journey, probably between the winter of 53 and the fall of 55. The main problems at Corinth were not those of Jew-Gentile relations, but those likely to arise in any big worldly city— sexual looseness, emotional excesses, church factions and quar-

---

[6] Gal. 2:16, A.S.V.
[7] Gal. 2:20, A.S.V.
[8] Gal. 3:28, R.S.V.
[9] Gal. 5:22, 23, A.S.V.

rels extending even to a serious attack on Paul's own leader-ship. It is practically certain that Paul wrote four letters to the Corinthians; first a letter on sexual immorality, lost to us except that a fragment may be preserved in II Corinthians 6:14—7:1 where the train of thought is interrupted by this passage[10]; then our present I Corinthians; then a sharp letter, the body of which is probably in II Corinthians 10—13, which Paul says he wrote "out of much affliction and anguish of heart . . . with many tears;"[11] then II Corinthians 1—9 in a mood of rejoicing after Titus had brought him the good news that the trouble had been settled. Nothing Paul wrote shows his great gifts as a pastor more clearly than these letters, and his words on spiritual gifts in I Corinthians 12 and 13 and his ode to immortality in I Corinthians 15 are among the finest things in all literature.

Romans.—After writing the Corinthian letters, Paul left Ephesus and journeyed to Macedonia and thence to Corinth, where he wrote the letter to the Romans, probably in 56. Paul had never been in Rome, the church there having been founded, so tradition has it, by Peter, though actually we do not know by whom. Paul thought that he ought to carry the gospel to Spain, but he planned to visit Rome on the way, both to encourage the Christians there and to establish a base from which to do his missionary work in the west. It was this anticipated visit that prompted the letter. It is naturally less personal than those written to people he knew, and it is his greatest theological statement—an exposition of his faith,

---

[10] Read II Cor. 6 and 7 without this passage and note how much more smoothly it fits together.

[11] II Cor. 2:4

its foundations, its bearing on suffering, sin, and problems of moral decision. Its primary theme is justification by faith. Neither the wisdom of the Greeks nor the law of the Jews can save a man; it is only as one recognizes his sinfulness and through faith finds victory in Christ that true peace is found. In chapter seven there is a wonderfully vivid description, probably autobiographical, of the futility of good intentions to master temptation, and this is followed by a paean of victory through Christ, in Romans 8, which rivals I Corinthians 13 in beauty and power. Though Paul had no use for what we now call moralism—the reliance on one's own good works—he gave great importance to Christian morality, and this is found at his best in the compendium of ethical injunctions in Romans 12—15.

Paul did get to Rome, but not in the way he had expected. Going to Jerusalem first, to take some relief funds from the churches visited to the Christians at Jerusalem, he there was arrested, kept in prison in Caesarea for two years, and upon appealing to Caesar was sent as a prisoner to Rome. The Book of Acts is tantalizing in scarcity of details as to the outcome, and stops with the report of his living in his own hired house for two years, preaching and teaching unhindered. It is generally believed that he was executed by command of the emperor Nero, probably in the year 64. From this period of Roman imprisonment are to be dated the letters to the Colossians, to Philemon, to the Philippians, and perhaps that to the Ephesians.

Colossians and Ephesians.—The Epistles to the Colossians and to the Ephesians are much alike, so much so that some scholars believe that Colossians was written by Paul, and Ephesians by someone later in imitation. However, in the absence of evidence to the contrary the Pauline authorship is still a real probability. Do not you and I sometimes write almost the same thing to different persons? The theme of the letters is twofold: the cosmic significance of Christ, and the duties demanded of Christian wives and husbands, children and parents, servants and masters. At least in the case of the letter to the Colossians, the occasion was the outcropping of the heresy of Gnosticism by which Christ was made simply one of many intermediate powers between God and man. This church at Colossae, a hundred miles east of Ephesus, was never visited by Paul, but he was concerned about the Christian groups everywhere. The letter to the Ephesians contains not only a tribute to the supreme and unique place of Christ, but also a beautiful prayer and benediction in Ephesians 3:14-21 and a noble passage in the sixth chapter on "the whole armor of God."

Philemon.—The Book of Philemon, consisting of only one chapter, is the shortest of Paul's letters, but priceless. It is a purely personal letter from one Christian to another about a third. Onesimus, a runaway slave with whom Paul had become acquainted at Rome, is here commended to his master Philemon with the hope expressed "for love's sake" that Philemon will receive him "no longer as a servant, but more than a servant, a brother beloved . . . both in the flesh and in the Lord."[12]

Philippians.—The letter to the Philippians is probably Paul's last. It breathes a spirit of tenderness and of gratitude

---

[12] Philemon vs. 16

both for their gifts to him and their fidelity to Christ. But more than all, its keynote is joy. Consider that Paul was in prison, facing death, and this farewell message becomes a deeply moving evidence of his own spiritual triumph.

> Rejoice in the Lord always; again I will say, Rejoice. Let all men know your forbearance. The Lord is at hand. Have no anxiety about anything, but in everything by prayer and supplication with thanksgiving let your requests be made known to God. And the peace of God, which passes all understanding, will keep your hearts and your minds in Christ Jesus.[13]

General Observations.—From this brief survey two things must be evident. The first is that Paul, having no idea he was writing Scripture, dealt with whatever situation called forth a letter. It was farthest from his thought that his injunction to the Corinthian women not to make themselves conspicuous,[14] or his observation to the Romans that "the powers that be are ordained of God,"[15] would be taken nineteen centuries later as a bulwark of conservatism. Indeed, such a use is quite the antithesis of his observation that "where the Spirit of the Lord is, there is liberty."[16] Many statements in his letters are situation-conditioned, and can be properly understood only in relation to the situation that evoked them.

Our second observation is the vast amount of permanent truth he expressed. He seems to have had an instinct—or shall we say, a gift of the Spirit—for taking any situation however sordid and saying something that would ring through the ages to inspire us. For example, some of the Corinthian Christians

---

[13] Phil. 4:4, R.S.V.
[14] I Cor. 14:34, 35
[15] Rom. 13:1
[16] II Cor. 3:17

were making pigs of themselves at the Lord's table, and he uses this incident to pen the marvelous words in I Corinthians 11:23-26 which we still use in our ritual. There was a dispute as to what kind of activity in the Church was most important, and he used it as the occasion to give a great interpretation of "the Body of Christ."[17] It is no accident that, through the centuries, so many millions have found inspiration in Paul's vibrant faith and spiritual wisdom.

THE GOSPELS AND ACTS

All these letters were written before any of the historical records in the New Testament were compiled. From them we get a good deal of information about Paul and the early Church, but very little about Jesus. Why did not Paul say more about our Lord's life and teaching? The answer is twofold. For one reason, his own interest was so centered in the new life in Christ through our Lord's death, resurrection, and living presence as the Spirit, that he did not focus attention on the details of Jesus' life and teaching. For another, the memory of Jesus was so fresh that the events of his life and his sayings did not seem to need recounting. We may well believe that Paul's message would have been greater if he had put more of Jesus' life and teaching into it. But we cannot expect everything of one person.

The earliest of our Gospels is Mark, written between 65 and 70, very soon after the death of Paul. Indeed, the shock of the persecutions under Nero may have prompted a sense of need for a more complete written record, though this is also to be explained by the fact that those who had known

---

[17] I Cor. 12

Jesus personally were gone or going, and oral tradition was no longer enough. As Paul had put it, "Even though we have known Christ after the flesh, yet now we know him so no more."[18]

But what had been happening in the meantime? The combination of the poetic form in which many of Jesus' sayings were cast, the vitality of his utterance, and the wonder and marvel of his deeds had caused these teachings and stories to be repeated over and over, not only privately, but also in the services and instruction of the churches. Some of them were undoubtedly written down, here and there, by unknown hands. Then these reports, mainly of Jesus' sayings but with some narrative material, were compiled into a written record earlier than Mark's. We do not know its author and it is now lost except as we have it in the excerpts Matthew and Luke took from it; yet it certainly once existed, and we call it "Q" from the German word *Quelle,* meaning source.

How can we be so sure it existed? Mark's Gospel is mainly narrative, with Jesus' teachings incidental to the story. The Gospel of Matthew, which was written between 70 and 80, and that of Luke, five or ten years later, apparently borrowed from Mark, for they follow his general pattern as to the events of Jesus' ministry. But they contain also a great deal of teaching material, such as the Sermon on the Mount and many parables, which Mark does not give. What they report is too nearly identical to be explained in any other way except that they both had access to a collection of Jesus' sayings. No New Testament scholar now doubts the existence

---

[18] II Cor. 5:16, A.S.V.

of "Q" though some believe that still other written sources
were drawn upon.

We speak of the first three Gospels as the Synoptic Gospels
because this word means "seen from one view," and there are
great similarities in them. The Gospel of John, written a
good deal later than these, is different in structure, style, and
quite largely in content. We must now take a look at what
is distinctive about each.

Mark.—The Gospel of Mark was probably written in Rome
shortly before the destruction of Jerusalem in the year 70. The
Christian bishop Papias, writing about 140, states: "Mark who
was the interpreter of Peter wrote accurately but not in order
all that he remembered of what Christ said and did. For he
did not hear the Lord or accompany him, but was later, as I
said, a companion of Peter. . . ." [19] While it is not certain
that Mark's Gospel is thus based on Peter's memories, it is
possible. Peter as well as Paul is believed to have lost his life
at Rome in the persecutions under Nero, and it is likely that
John Mark, who is mentioned both in the Book of Acts and in
Paul's letters as traveling with Paul, Barnabas, and Peter, is
the author of this record.

Several things are notable about this earliest Gospel. It
plunges directly into the events of Jesus' baptism and ministry,
with no reference to his birth or parentage. This is evidence
that the story of a virgin birth was not current at the time, for
Mark makes much of the miraculous to attest Jesus' supernatural power, and he would surely have reported a miraculous

---

[19] From *The Ecclesiastical History,* Eusebius; trans., H. J. Lawlor and
J. E. L. Oulton. New York: The Macmillan Company, 1927, Vol. I,
Bk. III, p. 39.

birth if he had known of it. The Gospel throughout is characterized by its vigor, its directness—with many a "straightway" introducing a new scene—its graphic pictorial touches, its unstudied but powerful drama. It moves to a climax in Peter's great confession at Caesarea Philippi,[20] and on to the tragic events of passion week. Mark's omission of any reference to Peter's being given the keys of the Kingdom is again significant. More than a third of the whole is given to the events of Jesus' last week in Jerusalem, which shows what he certainly thought to be most important. All the earliest manuscripts end at Mark 16:8. The original ending has apparently been lost and a spurious one added by some later hand.

Matthew.—The Gospel of Matthew is generally believed to have been written at Antioch in Syria, the city in which the disciples were first called Christians.[21] In any case it was compiled by some Jewish Christian with a strong desire both to show that at every point Jesus fulfilled the prophecies of the Jewish Scriptures and that he had a message and mission to the Gentiles because the Jews had rejected him. The writer certainly had access both to "Q" and Mark, and possibly to a collection of the sayings of Jesus compiled by the disciple Matthew, which may be responsible for its being called the Gospel according to Matthew.

What stands out in Matthew, in addition to its Jewish slant, is the orderly way in which the author groups the discourses of Jesus. He gives us five blocks of such teachings: (1) the Sermon on the Mount in chapters 5—7; (2) the directions to the disciples in chapter 10; (3) a group of parables about

---

[20] Mark 8:27-34   [21] Acts 11:26

the Kingdom in chapter 13; (4) parables and sayings about Christian behavior in the Kingdom, chapter 18; (5) and more parables about the coming of the Kingdom in chapters 24 and 25. It is unlikely that Jesus spoke all these discourses so connectedly, but the author, with an eye to topical arrangement, intersperses the "Q" material where it seems to fit the narrative from Mark. We owe him a great debt also for his literary gifts, for what might have been a mere piecing together is a unified whole in which one feels that Jesus' poetic, moving diction has been marvelously preserved.

Luke-Acts.—Our next Gospel, that of Luke, is half of a longer book often referred to as Luke-Acts, the first part being the story of Jesus, the second of the spread of the gospel and the birth of the Church. Not only are both parts addressed to the same man, Theophilus, with a reference at the beginning of Acts to the author's "first book," but also the style of writing is remarkably similar. Though apparently written in a continuous sequence, the two parts were separated early in the second century so that the Gospel section could be placed with the other three Gospels to form a fourfold story of Jesus. Though both are beautifully and vividly written, Acts is perhaps the more indispensible since it contains our only knowledge, outside of incidental references in Paul's letters, of those extremely vital events when the Church was coming into being.

Who was Luke? He was the friend and companion of Paul, referred to as "the beloved physician."[22] That considerable portions of Acts are based on his travel diary is evidenced by the "we" sections toward the end of the book, where the story

---

[22] Col. 4:14

is told in the first person.[23] For the Gospel, he, like Matthew, had access to "Q," Mark, and possibly other fragments; for Acts, besides his diary and personal memories, he doubtless had some records of happenings at Jerusalem before the missionary journeys started. The story, however, is his own graphic narrative, written probably between 85 and 95, and for the express purpose, he says, of giving an orderly and accurate account of what had happened.[24]

Each of the Gospel writers has his own particular merits. What stands out in Luke are the depth of his human sympathies, his sense of wonder, amazement, and joy at the power of the gospel, his poetic insight which led him not only to tell the Christmas story in a way that captivates old and young alike after nineteen centuries, but also to incorporate such lovely poems as the "Magnificat" of Mary, Zachariah's "Benedictus," and Simeon's "Nunc Dimittis."[25] With a few deft strokes and the inclusion of some apparently minor details, he could tell a story so that we see it before our eyes. as in the story of the boy Jesus in the Temple, or Jesus' first sermon and the anger of his townsmen afterwards, or the death of Stephen, or the shipwreck where Paul is master of the scene.[26] A glance at some of the parables found only in Luke shows how deeply we are indebted to him for words of Jesus that go to the heart of human relations—the Good Samaritan, the Prodigal Son, the Pharisee and the Publican, the Rich Man and Lazarus. Furthermore, Jesus

---

[23] These sections are Acts 16:10-17; 20:5-15; 21-1-18; 27:1—28:16. Note how smoothly, with no change in style, the author alternates between "we" and "they."

[24] Luke 1:1-4

[25] Luke 1:45, 55, 68-79; 2:29-35

[26] Luke 2:41-51; 4:16-30; Acts 7:54-60; 27:9-44

himself is here portrayed not so much as the fulfillment of messianic prophecy as actuated by divine compassion for the sinful, the sick, the poor, the outcast—all sorts of people. The glow and marvel of the new life through Christ, whether in Jesus' lifetime or in the early Church, must have captured Luke, for through his words it captures us today.

John.—In looking at the Gospel of John we must take a jump ahead in time sequence, beyond the books emerging from persecution which we shall discuss in the next section, into the early second century. It was probably written at Ephesus between 100 and 110, though possibly a little before or after this period. Who wrote it? We do not know, but there is little likelihood that the author was John the beloved disciple. John 21:20-24 appears to say so. But the book ended originally with chapter 20, and the last chapter is a sort of postscript added by someone who thought that John the disciple wrote it. The most we can be sure of is that it was written by some deeply religious soul, probably a Greek, and certainly one very familiar with Greek philosophy, who wanted to interpret for the Gentile world the spiritual significance of Christ and the Christian faith. Whoever wrote it, its message is undying.

Is the book authentic? This depends on what we mean by "authentic." It is less accurate factual history than is found in the three earlier Gospels. But it fulfills marvelously the author's purpose as he states it at the original ending in John 20:31, "These are written that you may believe that Jesus is the Christ, the Son of God, and that believing you may have life in his name." As early as the third century Clement of Alexandria spoke of this book as a "spiritual gospel," and this it has been through the centuries as Christians have loved it and been moved by it to greater inward depths.

The Gospel of John has three main sections. The first is the beautiful prologue in John 1:1-14, in which Jesus is presented as the incarnate Logos, "the Word made flesh" to dwell among us in undying light, "full of grace and truth." The remainder of the first twelve chapters presents incidents from the life of Jesus in which his supernatural powers are evident, and the people, seeing his wonderful works, believe. Chapters thirteen and onward contain the great last supper discourse and the events of the crucifixion and resurrection. In contrast to the Synoptics, Jesus here repeatedly asserts his oneness with the Father. There is no wilderness temptation, no agony in Gethsemane; Jesus without struggle is in command of every situation. This picture doubtless reflects what the Church had come to believe some seventy years after his death. But in any case, the book is a matchless treasury of Christian devotion cast in moving biography, full of such vivifying truth as the meaning of eternal life and the coming of the Spirit, the promised Comforter. To read it is to drink of the Water of Life it proclaims our Lord to be.

THE LITERATURE OF PERSECUTION

Practically from the beginning, Christianity met with persecution. There were outbursts from the Jews, such as actuated Paul before his conversion and led to the death of Stephen, and as these subsided the Romans persecuted the emerging sect. We have already said that probably Peter and Paul both died under Nero. But it was not until the end of the century, under Domitian who reigned from 81 to 96, that persecution became general throughout the Roman Empire. He demanded that divine honors be paid to him as a symbol of loyalty, and those Christians who refused to place incense before his statue were branded as traitors to the State. Three books in the New Testament written in the decade between 85 and 95 reflect this conflict: Hebrews, Revelation, and I Peter.

Hebrews.—We do not know who wrote the Epistle to the Hebrews, but we can be sure that it was not Paul. It does not "read like him" at all. It is written in a grand oratorical manner, more like a sermon than a letter, though it ends with a personal greeting. Many believe that it was written by a leader of the church at Rome who, while away from there, wrote out and sent by a messenger the sermon he would have liked to preach. It is called Hebrews because Christ is presented as the great high priest "after the order of Melchizedek,"[27] and Christianity, as a faith that completes and supersedes Judaism. Its climax is reached in a marvelous roll call of the heroes of faith, and the summons, because we are "compassed about with so great a cloud of witnesses," to "run with patience the race that is set before us, looking unto Jesus the author and perfecter of our faith."[28]

Revelation.—The Book of Revelation (not Revelations, as it is often incorrectly called) is one of the hardest books in the Bible to understand. Though nothing can make it perfectly simple, knowledge of its setting and type of literature can help greatly. It is apocalyptic writing, of which we noted a sample

---

[27] In Hebrews 7 Melchizedek is referred to as contemporary with Abraham but without beginning or end of life. This suggests the eternal foundations of Jesus' high priesthood.

[28] Heb. 11:1—12·2, A.S.V.

in Daniel and of which there was much in the period between the Testaments. Apocalyptic literature follows the pattern of a vision in which the author receives a call to write, and then describes, with highly cryptic imagery, a series of symbolic events which predict the overthrow of evil and the triumph of righteousness. It often appeared in times of crisis when its author could not speak openly. The Christians of the first century were much more familiar with this type of writing than we are, and hence much that puzzles us was clear to them.

The Book of Revelation is the apocalypse of John—what John we do not know except that he wrote from the island of Patmos, where he had probably been exiled for his faith. The writing dates from the end of the Domitian persecutions, about 95. The churches addressed at the beginning are seven, near Ephesus, but it is apparently written for the Church at large, as a message of warning but still more of encouragement in the midst of their sufferings. There is vivid dramatic contrast, in the visions that follow, between the terrors that stalk the earth—strife, famine, invasion, death, fire, flood, hail, earthquake, drought, pestilence, war—and the mighty chorus of adoration and worship of Christ, the Lamb who was slain for our redemption. This contrast appears also with great poignancy in the description of the utter destruction that will fall upon Rome, which the author identifies with Babylon, "the beast," a "great harlot" drunk with the blood of the saints, and the blessedness of the new heaven and the new earth which God has in store for his faithful ones. The main motif of the book is summed up for the individual in "Be thou faithful unto death, and I will give thee the crown of life;"[29] and for all society in

---

[29] Rev. 2:10, A.S.V.

The kingdom of the world has become the kingdom
our Lord and of his Christ, and he shall reign for ever
and ever.[30]

I Peter.—Very soon after, a letter was addressed in quite a
different vein to the churches of Asia Minor. This is called
I Peter, though Peter the disciple was long since dead. It is a
choice gem of practical Christian wisdom. Instead of adopting
an antagonistic attitude toward Rome, its author's counsel is,
"Honor all men. Love the brotherhood. Fear God. Honor
the king."[31] But he is well aware of the "fiery trials" his fellow
Christians are passing through, and he urges them to remain
steadfast, remembering that they are partakers of Christ's sufferings. There is a lovely suggestion of the difference Christ makes,
"who called you out of darkness into his marvelous light. Once
you were no people but now you are God's people."[32] They
are so to live that they will be witnesses of their faith.

OTHER NEW TESTAMENT BOOKS

We must take a concluding, rapid look at the rest of the New
Testament books. All are letters but one, the Book of James.

James.—James is a sermon—an excellent sermon—full of
Christian moral advice and exhortation. The author picks out
exactly the things that tempt us today—thinking too well of
ourselves, showing partiality, kowtowing to wealth, talking too
much—and warns against them. There is little to indicate its
date, except that the author seems to blend the Jewish wisdom
literature as found in Proverbs with the style of the Cynic and
Stoic traveling preachers. It was probably written toward the

---

[30] Rev. 11:15, R.S.V.   [32] I Pet. 2:9, 10, R.S.V.
[31] I Pet. 2:17

end of the first century or the early part of the second, after Christianity was well established in the Greek world.

I, II, and III John.—We noted the devotional qualities of the Gospel of John. The three letters that we call I, II, and III John are so much in the same mood that they may have been written by the same person who wrote the Gospel, though we cannot be sure. (Note how utterly different in style and theme from the John who wrote the Book of Revelation.) Their author writes to warn the churches against false teachings, particularly the claims of entire sanctification and the Gnostic heresies asserting a special illumination, which were upsetting them and causing divisions. His way of doing it is to stress the importance of love and the genuine spiritual illumination that flowers in right ethical living.

Jude and II Peter.—The Epistles of Jude and II Peter deal with the same problem of heresy as I, II, and III John, but in a very different mood—denunciatory and unloving. They are so much alike that in all probability the author of II Peter took Jude and incorporated it into his own writing. Second Peter is pseudepigraphic; that is, it is put out in the name of Simon Peter the apostle though not written by him. This was a common practice to secure a better hearing, not considered dishonest any more than the use of a pen name now. These books are historically important because they throw light on the dissensions that emerged as the churches, a century after Jesus' death, were solidifying into an ecclesiastical system. They do not give us so much in the way of personal inspiration—not even much positive statement of the faith which, Jude says, "was once for all delivered to the saints."[33]

---

[33] Jude vs. 3, R.S.V.

I and II Timothy and Titus.—We have nearly finished. The three Pastoral Epistles, I and II Timothy and Titus, are important but problematic books. Clearly they were all written by the same hand. Was this hand Paul's? Not only the fact that Timothy and Titus were Paul's co-workers, but also a number of intimate touches make it seem so. But when the letters as a whole are carefully examined it seems more likely that they were written in the middle of the second than of the first century. They assume not only a settled ecclesiastical system in the Church, but also an established body of orthodox beliefs against which to judge heresy and, what is most significant, a collection of Christian Scriptures. Perhaps some notes of Paul's were incorporated, somewhat as the Gospel writers drew on earlier sources, but it is practically certain that these letters in their finished form stand at or near the end of the New Testament writings.

Whoever wrote them, they have their own great merits. They deal with the training of leaders for local churches and with the Christian duties not only of these leaders but also of church members. Though some statements here are situation-conditioned, there is much that still speaks to us in our time. Such passages as "I permit no woman to teach or to have authority over men; she is to keep silent,"[34] we can let pass as a vestige of an earlier day; in such injunctions as "Let no one despise your youth. . . . Do not neglect the gift you have. . . . Take heed to yourself and to your teaching,"[35] there is eternal wisdom.

And such a blending we have found throughout the New Testament and the Old. In the Bible is a great treasury of wisdom from God. "But," as Paul puts it in speaking of the light

---

[34] I Tim. 2:12, R.S.V.   [35] I Tim. 4:12, 14, 16, R.S.V.

that shines from God in Christ, "we have this treasure in earthen vessels, to show that the transcendent power belongs to God and not to us."[36] If this survey of the earthen vessels through which God has revealed himself in the Bible has not made clearer the heavenly treasure, these chapters will have missed their aim.

---

[36] II Cor. 4:7, R.S.V.

CHAPTER FIVE

The Great Ideas of the Bible

In the third and fourth chapters we traced how the Bible came to be written, over a period which stretches from the tenth century before Christ to the second century after, in the midst of widely varying situations. We have seen how different types of literature emerged out of differing circumstances and out of the diverse purposes and temperaments of the authors. We have noted its "infinite variety," which, to adapt the words of Shakespeare, "age cannot wither, nor custom stale." It must be evident by now that to put the Bible all on one level, to be accepted or rejected without regard to what each particular author is trying to say, is not only to do violence to the historical method but also to lose much of the great spiritual truth and meaning God is seeking to have us grasp.

But now appears an important paradox. The Bible is sixty-six books; yet it is one book, and has been so considered and read for many centuries. The Bible expresses many ideas; yet it all centers around one great idea. This grand theme, which runs throughout the Bible and binds it into a unity, is the activity of the living God.

This activity of the living God takes many forms. He creates, commands, rebukes, judges, forgives, redeems, guides, enlightens, strengthens, consoles, saves, and delivers his people. There is no single way in which he does this, though there is a great central unity in his sending his Son Jesus Christ to be the Way, the Truth, and the Life. But what the Bible deals with throughout, and what Christian theology must deal with if it takes its rise as it should from the Bible, is this work of the living God in human history.

What we shall attempt in this chapter is to discover the biblical basis for our Christian faith in God, and then suggest the bearing of this faith on certain other great convictions of our Christian heritage.

God

We have spoken of the *"living* God." Why call him this? Certainly not because he has biological life such as we have in our physical bodies. Though he is spoken of anthropomorphically (as a being in human form) at some points in the Bible, particularly in the early "J" stories of the Old Testament, this is not the normal biblical understanding of his nature. Rather, the great affirmation attributed to Jesus in the Fourth Gospel, "God is spirit, and those who worship him must worship in spirit and truth,"[1] is presupposed throughout the greater part of the Bible.

We speak of the living God to stress what in more philosophical language is called a personal God—one who loves and cares, who thinks and wills, who created the world and who continuously acts within it. This becomes clearer in contrast with what God is not. Most of the religions and many of the philosophies of the world have had a Supreme Being as their center, and God has been variously thought of as the Highest

---

[1] John 4:24, R.S.V.

Good, or the Unmoved Mover, or the First Cause, or the Absolute in whom all contradictions are reconciled, or an impersonal cosmic force or process at work in the world, or the personification and projection outward of man's own high impulses. Biblical faith, on the contrary, is centered in the existence and activity of a deity who is infinite in wisdom, power, and love, but who nevertheless cares personally for each of us, a God whom we can approach in prayer and from whom we can receive help and strength, a God who is always acting within the human scene and is known to us by his acts. The "God and Father of our Lord Jesus Christ" is never a philosophical abstraction nor an impersonal force; he is the living God on whom our lives depend.

The existence of this God is never argued about in the Bible; we find nowhere a list of proofs. His reality is simply affirmed, and all the rest of the Bible hinges on this great affirmation. The idea of Yahweh, as we have seen, grew in the minds of the Hebrews from the conviction that, though there were other gods, supreme loyalty was owed to him, on to the clear-cut universal monotheism of the Second Isaiah. But during this development, and later, there is surprisingly little change in what was believed about the nature of God himself. There are shifts of emphasis, as from God's relation to the nation, which predominates in the Old Testament, to his loving care for each individual in Jesus' favorite symbol of God as Father. Whereas God's covenant with Israel stands out in his dealings with the "chosen people" in the Old Testament, his revelation of himself in Jesus and his presence as Holy Spirit in the Christian fellowship are central in the New. But while these changes in emphasis appear, it is still the same God "yesterday, today and forever," who is worshiped, prayed to, feared, trusted, and in some measure obeyed.

The central categories around which the biblical writers conceived of God—though of course never in a formal systematic classification such as we must use for convenience in analysis—are as Creator, Judge, Redeemer, Father. Let us see what is implied in each of these terms.

As Creator

That *God is the Creator* is affirmed in the first verse of the Bible. The majestic account of creation found in Genesis 1:1— 2:4 is in the "P" literature; hence we conclude that it was written late. Nevertheless what it affirms about the transcendent power of God to bring the world into being by his will, and call it good, is presupposed much earlier. The biblical writers were not concerned, as we have to be, with scientific processes. What they were concerned about was the holiness of God. When Isaiah in the temple vision heard the seraphim crying to one another, "Holy, holy, holy, is the Lord of hosts: the whole earth is full of his glory,"[2] this hymn of praise to God's glory reflected the prevalent idea about God's relation to his world. There is less said in the Bible about creation than either judgment or redemption. Yet it did not occur to the biblical writers to doubt that this is God's world, and many times they affirmed it, as in Second Isaiah's grateful and joyous exclamation:

> Hast thou not known? hast thou not heard? The everlasting God, the Lord, the Creator of the ends of the earth, fainteth not, neither is weary; there is no

___
[2] Isa. 6:3

searching of his understanding. He giveth power to the
faint; and to him that hath no might he increaseth
strength,[3]

or the psalmist's paean:

> The heavens declare the glory of God;
> And the firmament showeth his handiwork,[4]

or Jesus' calm assurance that the God who feeds the birds of the
air, clothes the lilies of the field, and makes his sun to shine and
his rain to fall, will do for us what we need.[5]

This biblical certainty of God as the Creator ought to mean
a number of things to us. It means, obviously, that whatever
science may tell us about the processes by which creation takes
place, science can never take the place of the Lord of heaven
and earth by whose wisdom and power the processes were
initiated and continue. It means, furthermore, that we ought not
simply to think of the Creator as a First Cause who started
things, but that like the biblical writers we too are obligated to
bow in reverent awe before "the high and lofty One that in-
habiteth eternity, whose name is Holy."[6] The more we learn
about our world, the more we should be prompted to exclaim
with the psalmist,

> Wonderful are thy works;
> And that my soul knoweth right well.[7]

Creation means that contemplation of the majesty of God's
work and the holiness of the Creator ought to make us very
humble about ourselves, remembering that he still says to us, as
to the people of Israel:

---

[3] Isa. 40:28, 29, A.S.V. [5] Matt. 5:45; 6:26-30 [7] Ps. 139:14, A.S.V
[4] Ps. 19:1, A.S.V. [6] Isa. 57:15

> For my thoughts are not your thoughts, neither are
> your ways my ways. . . . For as the heavens are higher
> than the earth, so are my ways higher than your ways,
> and my thoughts than your thoughts.[8]

In a secular age, when we are accustomed to take great pride
and place great confidence in what man can create by his own
knowledge and skill, such a reminder that we have not the
final wisdom is much in order. And finally, the awareness that
our existence and whatever we have are God's gifts, and whatever control we have over the world is a delegated responsibility
—in which, to use the Genesis phrase, God has made us to "have
dominion" over the things of nature—ought to give us a wider,
deeper sense of stewardship.

As Judge

The idea of *God as the righteous Judge* is in general harder
for the modern mind to grasp than that of God as the Creator.
Not that righteousness is hard to conceive of in God. If the
Bible says anything, it says that God is good, and righteousness
is another word for goodness. What we balk at in the idea of
judgment is the idea of sternness implied in it, and its association with punishment, wrath, and indignation. Also, though we
may not realize it, we do not like to think of ourselves as sinners who fall under God's righteous condemnation.

We have to move carefully here, and put together two basic
biblical ideas which, though they may seem contradictory on
the surface, are not, actually. It may be helpful to note what
mistakes arise if we do not keep them together.

---

[8] Isa. 55:8, 9, A.S.V. Note also the beautiful nature imagery which
follows.

In an earlier day, much was made of the wrath of God and his punishment of sinners both on earth and in the fires of hell. A desire "to flee from the wrath to come" was made a crucial test of Christian experience and even of church membership. Jonathan Edwards preached a famous sermon on "Sinners in the Hands of an Angry God." Then, because this did not seem to square with the loving Father God of Jesus, we swung completely around, and the goodness of God became a sort of sentimental benevolence. Also, with the advance of scientific achievement and progressive education, and a new psychological knowledge of human motivations and drives, the whole idea of sin fell into disrepute. Judgment went with it, and came to be thought of as an antiquated Old Testament idea, which we did not need any longer to accept.

Neither of these extremes is biblical, and neither is true to human experience. What the Bible teaches, throughout the Old Testament and the New, is that man is a rebellious sinner; that God cannot countenance sin; that he has to punish us to get us to mend our ways. These teachings run through the message of every one of the prophets. Furthermore, since God is the Lord of history, even the enemies of Israel could be used by Yahweh as the instruments of his righteous judgment. Others might think of the Day of the Lord as "sweetness and light" with prosperity just around the corner; not so the true spokesmen of Yahweh. Amos put it with tremendous vividness in his warnings against the people's boasted security:

> Woe unto you that desire the day of the Lord! to what end is it for you? the day of the Lord is darkness, and not light. As if a man did flee from a lion, and a bear met him; or went into the house, and leaned his hand on

the wall, and a serpent bit him. Shall not the day of the Lord be darkness, and not light? even very dark, and no brightness in it?[9]

While this message is less conspicuous in the New Testament, it is there. Not only did John the Baptist call his hearers to repentance because "the ax is laid to the root of the trees," but Jesus also preached, "Repent, for the kingdom of heaven is at hand."[10] In one of the most poignantly beautiful passages in the Gospels, Jesus, directly after his triumphal entry into Jerusalem, wept over the city because his countrymen were failing to see "the things which belong unto peace," and gave a terrible warning of impending disasters "because thou knewest not the time of thy visitation."[11]

But are such warnings in the mood of pure pessimism? Or do they reflect a vindictive deity? By no means. It is basic to the biblical idea of judgment that God punishes in order to redeem. "For whom the Lord loveth he chasteneth."[12] Judgment is linked throughout with the possibility and promise of salvation to those who repent and turn to God. "Seek the Lord, and ye shall live"[13] is as central to Amos' message as his warnings of doom. The positive side of judgment by a loving God has been marvelously expressed in the Gospel of John where the author says:

> For God so loved the world that he gave his only Son, that whoever believes in him should not perish but have eternal life. For God sent the Son into the world, not to condemn the world, but that the world might be saved

---

[9] Amos. 5:18-20
[10] Matt. 3:10;4:17, R.S.V.
[11] Luke 19:41-44, A.S.V.
[12] Heb. 12:6
[13] Amos 5:6. Note how warning and promise are interwoven in this chapter.

through him. . . . And this is the judgment, that the
light has come into the world, and men loved darkness
rather than light, because their deeds were evil.[14]

This biblical note of divine judgment has a particular pertin
ence in our own day, when so much chaos has come upon the
world because of personal and national sin and the flouting of
the ways of God revealed to us by the light of Christ. Even the
acts of enemy countries today, like those of Assyria and Rome,
may be used by God to bring judgment without his sharing
in their sin. But beneath every note of judgment found in
the Bible or in contemporary life must be seen, if we are
Christian, God's redeeming love and a divine sorrow that is
seeking always to save us from our folly and misdeeds.

As Redeemer

This brings us to *God as the Redeemer*. Herein lies the heart
of the biblical message.

The idea of God's saving mercy and help, which is what redemption means, is found throughout the Bible. Although other
notes are mixed in with it, including not only divine judgment
but also occasionally the attribution to God of petty anger and
jealousies and the need to be appeased, the main stream of the
Bible's message is of a God who loves men, even sinful men,
enough to yearn to save them from their sins.

The message of God's redeeming love is centered in four
great concepts which move into one another by a natural sequence. These are God's covenant with Israel, the promise of
the Messiah, the incarnation of God in Christ, and his presence

---

[14] John 3:16, 17, 19, R.S.V.

in the Christian Church as the Holy Spirit. Each of these is a very large idea at which we shall look briefly.

Israel's sense of nationhood, and of being a chosen people with a great destiny, begins with the establishment of the covenant. This is best dated from the time of Moses and the deliverance from Egypt, which makes Exodus a very important book. Possibly it goes back to Abraham as recorded in Genesis 17, though this is more likely a later adaptation of the patriarchal stories to the covenant idea. In any case, from the moment the people of Israel saw themselves as God's people, adopted by Yahweh not only for special favors but also for great demands, it made a difference that stamped their whole history. In this is rooted their sense of sin, not simply as ordinary infraction of the moral standards of a primitive society, but as rebellion against God and an affront to his holiness. In it is rooted also their trust in God through the worst vicissitudes of their struggle against nature, against their enemies, against strange gods that competed with Yahweh for their loyalty. This sense of God's lovingkindness and protecting care is the background of the way their history is told, of the messages of their prophets, and of the great poetry of devotion that we find in the Psalms.

Nevertheless, the people did not keep their side of the covenant. Even at the moment the covenant was being made between Yahweh and Moses on Mount Sinai, the people, under Aaron, set up a golden calf to worship, and only Moses' intercession, so the story says, prevented Yahweh from consuming them forthwith in anger.[15] This was only the beginning of a very long series of transgressions which displeased Yahweh and caused the prophets roundly to chide the people. But amazingly,

---

[15] Exod. 32

the more discerning the prophet the more clearly he saw the mercy of God and the promise of a deliverer shining through the darkness. Among the many passages which foreshadow the coming of such a messiah, these from Isaiah are among the earliest and most vivid:

> The people that walked in darkness have seen a great light: they that dwelt in the land of the shadow of death, upon them hath the light shined. . . .
> And there shall come forth a shoot out of the stock of Jesse, and a branch out of his roots shall bear fruit. And the Spirit of the Lord shall rest upon him, the spirit of wisdom and understanding, the spirit of counsel and might, the spirit of knowledge and of the fear of the Lord. . . .[16]

Then follows the picture of the righteous, peace-giving reign of such a deliverer, with God's promise to a war-weary world.

> They shall not hurt nor destroy in all my holy mountain; for the earth shall be full of the knowledge of the Lord, as the waters cover the sea.[17]

The coming of this Deliverer is what the New Testament is all about. Does the Old Testament directly predict the coming of Christ? Yes and no—and as so often happens, an extreme position on either side leaves out important truth. These messianic prophecies are certainly present in abundance, and looking back at them from the perspective of what we know about Jesus we see that he fits them wonderfully. But there is no inherent reason why he had to be born in Bethlehem, or be a descendant of David. If we trust the genealogy in both Matthew and Luke which traces his ancestry through Joseph's line,

[16] Isa. 9:2; 11:1, 2, A.S.V.   [17] Isa. 11:9

he was.[18] But his messiahship was not that of a political king, and although he was a loyal Jew his vision of God's universal love far transcends Judaism. Had not the gospel writers, particularly Matthew, inserted so often, "that it might be fulfilled which was spoken by the prophet," we might be less inclined to look for exact predictions and be captured rather by the wonder and glory of God's redeeming love which Jesus came to bear.

Then came the crucifixion, and the resurrection, and the establishment of the Christian community in the Church. He who gave as his parting word, "Lo, I am with you always, even unto the end of the world,"[19] was with them still. And he lives with us, as the Spirit of life and truth. Through him our lives are made over, and by his Spirit our spirits are nourished and led. Through him we have our best knowledge and approach to God the Redeemer, the Christlike God.

AS FATHER

The Bible, then, gives us the basis of our Christian doctrines of creation, judgment, and redemption. But what of Jesus' name for God, by which he taught us to pray, *"Our Father"?* The fact that he thought of God as Father led the early churches to do so, and through his example and the New Testament writings[20] it has become our most familiar and beloved word for God.

---

[18] Note that the two genealogies differ, Matthew tracing his descent from David through Solomon, and Luke through David's son Nathan. From David back to Abraham there is close agreement.

[19] Matt. 28:20, A.S.V.

[20] It is in most, but not all, of them. It occurs most often in the Gospel of John.

This it should be. No understanding of God that leaves out his fatherly love and care for all his children, and with it the implied brotherhood of all men, can be fully Christian. However, it stands in a special relation to the other three terms we have looked at, for it gathers up in one word the meaning of all of them. Like a father, but far beyond any human father in wisdom, power, goodness, and understanding love, God brings us into existence, disciplines us to live as we ought, forgives us when we go astray, and loves us enough to help us to go forward to more victorious living.

Besides summing up in one great word what the Bible is trying throughout to say, to call God Father, in addition, shifts the emphasis from God's concern for the nation to his love for the individual. God is referred to as Father very few times in the Old Testament,[21] and the rarity of its use there in contrast to its central place in Jesus' thought marks the difference between God's covenant with the chosen people and the new covenant, written in men's hearts and open to all men everywhere. It is no accident that the basic roots of democracy are in human brotherhood, and brotherhood is meaningless apart from the divine fatherhood. This we need to realize in a day when many people are trying to have the fruits of democracy without its roots.

The Christian View of Man

We come now to an aspect of biblical thought that is very important for us to understand, and to put in its right relation

---

[21] Note references in Hos. 11:1-4; Isa. 1:2; 63:16; Jer. 3:19; Ps. 89:26.

to modern ways of thinking. What does the Bible tell us about ourselves?

There is no point on which theologians are so much divided, and, in turn, no point on which Christian thinkers in general are so well agreed as over against the current naturalistic assumptions of the secular world. Even to state what the biblical view is, is to lay oneself open to the charge of being biased. But let us see.

Let us note, in the first place, that the Bible is opposed to the common idea that man is simply a complex physical organism, just like one of the lower animals except a little more intelligent. When the psalmist says,

> Man that is in honor, and understandeth not,
> Is like the beasts that perish,[22]

what he is emphasizing is not that man is like the beasts but rather that, being different, he ought to use rightly the honor and understanding God has given him. In such passages as:

> But there is a spirit in man,
> And the breath of the Almighty giveth them understanding,[23]

or the beautiful proverb:

> The spirit of man is the candle of the Lord,[24]

or the words of the creation story,

> And the Lord God formed man of the dust of the ground, and breathed into his nostrils the breath of life; and man became a living soul,[25]

a view is expressed which is radically different from the idea

[22] Ps. 49:20, A.S.V.   [24] Prov. 20:27
[23] Job 32:8, A.S.V.   [25] Gen. 2:7

that man is merely a biological organism with a complicated set of neutral reactions.

And in the second place, there is never any suggestion in the Bible that man, being mechanically determined by a complex set of forces in his heredity and environment, has to do what he does without any freedom of choice. He is often represented as acting under the power of God, and again as being mastered by temptation he cannot resist without God's power. He could be seized by an evil spirit, even by a legion of them, or be led and strengthened by the divine Spirit. But this is a very different thing from the current notion that man has no freedom of will because his every act and thought is determined by some previous element in a chain of natural causes. This idea would have been abhorrent to the biblical writers if they had thought of it, as of course they could not before the idea of a universal system of natural law had emerged. They would have repudiated it because it undermines the very thing they were most concerned about—man's moral responsibility before God.

On these points—the reality of the spiritual nature of man and the reality of at least a limited freedom of choice as basic to moral responsibility—there is large agreement among Christians. It is held on the authority not only of the Bible but also of our own observation and experience. Though the opposite is taught in some universities, this does not make it true.

But now we come to points on which Christians do not agree. There is a divergence, on the one hand, between the fundamentalists and the liberals, and on the other, between the liberals and the neo-orthodox. Though there are meeting points along the way, and the divergence is not so complete as is sometimes supposed, there are, nevertheless, real differences.

The fundamentalists, who hold to a literal interpretation of the Bible as the only way to think of it as inspired, take the Genesis account of creation as accurate history. The world, from this view, was made by God in six days, with the creation of Adam and Eve as the final act. The evidence presented by geology, biology, and anthropology that the earth has been billions of years in coming to its present form, and that man as the product of a long evolutionary process has been on earth at least half a million years, is rejected as contradicting the Bible. The liberals, on the other hand, accept gladly all that science can tell us about the *processes* of creation, but agree with their conservative friends in holding that God is the Creator, that man is made in the image of God, and, as God's supreme creation, is a living soul with a great, God-given responsibility to honor and obey him.

But where do the liberals and the neo-orthodox differ? They agree in viewing the creation stories as prescientific myths with great spiritual meaning. But they differ in that the neo-orthodox stress man's weakness and sinfulness, while the liberals stress the fact that man is made in the spiritual image of God and, as the child of God, is a creature of infinite worth and dignity. There is no absolute difference here, for both schools of thought hold that man is made by God for a high destiny, yet is always a sinner. There is, however, a large difference in emphasis, and this emphasis affects the views one holds about Christian education, evangelism, the possibility of appealing to love in social action, and many other things.

There is no space here to trace these consequences. What does the Bible say about man's sinfulness versus his dignity?

It affirms both elements so unmistakably that we ought to have no uncertainty in affirming both. Man's sinfulness and our tendency to rebel against God and follow "the devices and desires of our own hearts" is written on every page. Less is said about man's dignity and greatness, for the biblical writers were for the most part concerned to exalt the holiness of God, protest man's disobedience, and proclaim God's saving mercy. Yet it is certainly there: in God's great commission in Genesis 1:28; in passages such as those quoted on page 122 about man's spirit and in Paul's word to the Corinthians, "Do you not know that your body is a temple of the Holy Spirit within you, which you have from God?"[26]; in poetry of surpassing beauty where the greatness of God and man, his supreme creation, are affirmed together.

> When I consider thy heavens, the work of thy fingers,
> The moon and the stars, which thou hast ordained;
> What is man, that thou art mindful or him?
> And the son of man, that thou visitest him?
> For thou hast made him but little lower than God,
> And crownest him with glory and honor.
> Thou makest him to have dominion over the works of
>   thy hands;
> Thou hast put all things under his feet.[27]

Furthermore, it is not in any particular quotation, but in Jesus' continual assumption that man—*every* man, woman, and child—is infinitely precious in God's sight, that we find our surest clue to man's dignity and true greatness. We ought to be humble, knowing our own sin and weakness. We ought to be

---

[26] I Cor. 6:19, R.S.V.   [27] Ps. 8:3-6, A.S.V.

charitable, knowing the evil forces that play upon and within others. But we ought also to respect the native goodness and the infinite, God-given possibilities of every man. This we shall not do if we think meanly of those whom Jesus taught us, by a common prayer to our Father, to call his sons and our brothers.

Eternal Life

Another great note in Christian faith is the hope of eternal life. What the Bible says about it is not so clear or detailed as we could wish in our inquiring moments. It tells us, however, all we really need to know for our hope and comfort.

The idea of personal existence beyond the grave in any definite sense was a late development in Jewish thought, though apparently there was a belief in Sheol as a vague and shadowy place of departed spirits, good and bad alike. This is incorrectly translated "hell" in the King James Version. Toward the end of the Old Testament writing, but much more in the apocalyptic literature that emerged between the Testaments, the idea became current of a resurrection of the dead and a great last judgment, after which the faithful would be taken to dwell with God in heaven and the wicked consigned to eternal torment in hell. This was doubtless influenced by the Zoroastrian religion of the Persians though not entirely derived from it. It was the view commonly held in Jesus' day, the Pharisees believing in such a resurrection and the Sadducees rejecting it, and against this background the apocalyptic passages in Mark 13 and Matthew 25 become easier to understand.

Jesus apparently accepted in the main this popular belief. But with a difference. There is nothing fatalistic or pessimistic or showily spectacular in his words; his emphasis is on our need to be watchful, obedient, and concerned to show our love and faithfulness to God by helping our fellow men. Note the ethical setting of the judgment scene which reaches its climax in "Truly, I say to you, as you did it to one of the least of these my brethren, you did it to me."[28] If we do this, we can leave the rest in God's hands, for time and eternity.

It was Jesus' own resurrection, establishing the certainty that God was victor over sin and death, that did most to assure the early Christians of immortal life through his power. Since they were not concerned, as we have to be, about the relations of soul and body, resurrection meant to them God's continuance of the whole person. We are not obliged to think exactly as they did, and we may well believe that the body perishes while the soul lives on in the nearer presence of God. No greater words on this subject have ever been written than Paul's in I Corinthians 15, while the author of the Fourth Gospel cites in Jesus' farewell message great promises of peace and joy in God's eternal kingdom.[29] John's Gospel also makes much of eternal life as a *quality* of life—the life in God through the saving gift of Christ—which begins on earth and endures forever.

Some theologians insist that for the life beyond the grave we must use the word resurrection, as the Bible usually does, rather than immortality, lest we arrogantly claim it as a human right. This distinction seems unnecessary, provided we recognize, as Jesus did, that it comes as the gift of a loving God. If the God of Jesus exists, his children are assured of life everlasting; if he does not, then it could neither be certain nor such as to be desired.

---

[28] Matt. 25:31-46, R.S.V.

[29] Especially John 14:1-3 but implied throughout chapters 14—17.

Jesus the Son of God

We must use these last few pages for a theme in which the whole Bible finds its meaning and center—a theme for which there would not be pages enough, even if we were at the beginning of the book instead of at the end of it. The early Christians worshiping in the catacombs had the fish as their symbol because *ichthus,* the Greek word for fish, was what they got when they took the first letters of the words, "Jesus Christ, the Son of God, the Savior." That is what he was to them, and what he is to Christians in every age.

The particular doctrines we must look at are the incarnation, the cross, the resurrection, and Christ's continuing presence as the Holy Spirit. Opinions differ widely regarding these doctrines, and sometimes, unfortunately, Christians have become uncharitable toward other Christians holding different views. Even when one's faith is grounded in the Bible, latitude must be left for differences of interpretation. Yet, to a surprising extent, Christians do agree on certain great central truths.

The *incarnation* means that "the Word became flesh" to dwell among us. That is, God sent his Son to live among us as a man, to show us his will and way. Whether Jesus was miraculously born is a question the Bible does not clearly answer for us; for while there are beautiful stories of a virgin birth in both Matthew and Luke,[30] these writers trace the ancestry of Jesus through Joseph's line. Mark, the author of the earliest Gospel, does not mention the virgin birth, as he almost surely would have if he had known of it, and Paul and John, though very sure of Jesus' divinity, say nothing as to the manner of his birth. Jesus is

---

[30] Matt. 1:18-25; Luke 1:26-35

elsewhere referred to as "the carpenter's son," and this he was apparently in his lifetime thought to be.[31] But the evidence remains divided. This is a matter on which Christians will doubtless continue to differ, and tolerance is in order. Yet on the question of Jesus' divinity—of his being in a true and unique sense the Son of God—there is great agreement among Christians. This is what the incarnation means, and what really matters.

Was Jesus the Son of God and our Savior because God ordained that he should be? Or because he was perfectly sensitive to God's call, perfectly obedient to his will? The answer is, *Both*. Take out either the divine initiative or Jesus' freely chosen response, and much that is important fades out of the doctrine of the incarnation. The author of the Epistle to the Hebrews says that Jesus, the Son of God, can sympathize with our weakness because he was "in all points tempted like as we are, yet without sin."[32] Yet try to make him simply a great prophet who went about doing good, and much of the power goes out of Christian faith. We call him Lord, as we call God our Lord, because we feel that in him God spoke, in him God acted for our salvation.

Bearing in mind the sequence in which the New Testament books were written, what do we find as to the growth of the idea of the incarnation? In Paul's letters Jesus is not called God but the Son of God, this great fact being attested by his resurrection. This event loomed so large in Paul's mind that, unfortunately for later thought derived from him, he did not give much attention to Jesus' earthly life. Mark states that his purpose is to set forth "the beginning of the gospel of Jesus

---

[31] Matt. 13:55; Luke 2:27, 33 41, 43, 48; John 6:42
[32] Heb. 4:15

Christ, the Son of God," and he starts with Jesus' baptism. The next stage was to push the matter of his divine sonship back to his birth, as in Matthew and Luke. Not stopping there, John views Jesus as the pre-existent Logos, the agent of God in creation, and identifies him with God. It is not surprising that different interpretations have emerged as one or another of these biblical foundations has been stressed. Yet through them all shines the great conviction that in Jesus we see God, his supreme revelation and our divine Savior.

The doctrine of *the cross,* or of the atonement Jesus made for our sins by his death on the cross, is so connected with the incarnation that the two must be viewed together. There have been held in Christian history various views of the atonement that are not very satisfactory: that Christ's death was a ransom paid to the devil, that he had to die to propitiate the wrath of God or to uphold God's authority, that he is our substitute in paying the penalty for sin—or along another line, that his death was simply a good moral influence and example to us. Deeper and truer than any of these is the view that as God's Son he revealed the love of God and brought to us the saving power of God through his entire ministry, with his death on the cross the great climax and focal point. Our Christian faith centers in the conviction that "the Son of man came not to be ministered unto, but to minister, and to give his life a ransom for many." [33] This ransom is not be be thought of in any external sense but as reaching into the heart of God and the depths of our human plight. To save us from our sins and futility by showing us the way of love and giving us through Christ the power to love,

[33] Matt. 20:28

God gave his Son for our redemption. This is stated many times in the Bible but nowhere more vividly than in the great words of Paul, "He that spared not his own Son, but delivered him up for us all, how shall he not with him also freely give us all things?" [34]

After the cross, the *resurrection*. This, like the story of the crucifixion, is found in all four Gospels and is presupposed throughout the rest of the New Testament writings. There is nothing in the Bible we can be more sure *did* happen, though we shall never know exactly *what* happened. The transformation of the utter discouragement of the disciples into a flaming new hope and faith attest it. The numerous accounts of it vary in details, but all agree as to the great change which came over the disciples. What happened *in them* can be explained as mystical experiences, such as you and I sometimes have when we feel the real presence of Christ at the communion table or in some great moment. But what caused them to have these experiences is inexplicable unless the resurrection really occurred. In the faith that Christ had risen victorious over sin and death, the Church was born, and in this conviction it has found power through all the ages since.

And now, finally, what does this mean to us? In John's Gospel there is a beautiful promise of the sending of the *Holy Spirit* to take the place of the earthly presence of Christ.

> These things have I spoken to you, while I am still with you. But the Counselor, the Holy Spirit, whom the Father will send in my name, he will teach you all things, and bring to your remembrance all that I have said to you. [35]

---

[34] Rom. 8:32   [35] John 14:25, 26, R.S.V.

The Book of Acts opens with the disciples tarrying in Jerusalem for the coming of the Holy Spirit, and then being filled with a great new flood of joy and power on the day of Pentecost. From then on, there was no doubt about the vitality of that little band of Christians, a fellowship with a gospel which eventually was to encompass the earth.

We are the inheritors of that little company. We have the same God, the same Christ, the same Holy Spirit they had. We have what they did not have—a body of Christian Scriptures in which the teachings and "mighty works" of Jesus are recorded. What shall we do with them? God is with us today to enlighten our minds, to quicken our wills, to stir our spirits by his Holy Spirit, that we may be taught in the things of Christ and led more steadfastly to live as his disciples.

Bibliography

HELPFUL BOOKS IN STUDYING THE BIBLE

I. COMMENTARIES:

Buttrick, George. (ed.). *The Interpreter's Bible*. New York: Abingdon-Cokesbury Press, 1951.

Dummelow, J. R. (ed.). *A Commentary on the Holy Bible*. New York: The Macmillan Co., 1947.

Eiselin, F. C.; Lewis, Edwin; and Downey, D. G. (ed.). *The Abingdon Bible Commentary*. New York: Abingdon Press, 1929.

Miller, Madeline S. and J. Lane. *Harper's Bible Dictionary*. New York: Harper & Bros., 1952.

II. GENERAL INTRODUCTIONS TO THE STUDY OF THE BIBLE:

Anderson, Bernhard W. *Rediscovering the Bible*. New York: Association Press, 1951.

Blair, Edward P. *The Bible and You*. New York: Abingdon-Cokesbury Press, 1953.

Bowie, W. R. *The Story of the Bible*. New York: Abingdon Press, 1935.

————. *The Bible*. New York: Association Press, 1939.

Chase, Mary Ellen. *The Bible and the Common Reader*. New York: The Macmillan Co., 1944.

Colwell, Ernest C. *The Study of the Bible*. New York: Cambridge University Press, 1937.

Dodd, C. H. *The Bible Today*. New York: Cambridge University Press, 1946.

Fosdick, Harry Emerson. *The Modern Use of the Bible*. New York: The Macmillan Co., 1924, 1940.

————. *A Guide to Understanding the Bible*. New York: Harper & Bros., 1938.

Goodspeed, Edgar J. *The Story of the Bible*. Chicago: University of Chicago Press, 1936. (Old and New Testaments are also available separately.)

————. *How to Read the Bible*. Philadelphia: John C. Winston Co., 1946.

Love, Julian P. *How to Read the Bible*. New York: The Macmillan Co., 1945.

BIBLIOGRAPHY

Mould, Elmer W. K. *Essentials of Bible History.* Revised. New
York: Ronald Press Co., 1951.
————. *Bible History Digest.* New York: Exposition Press,
1950.
Parmelee, Alice. *A Guidebook to the Bible.* New York: Harper
& Bros., 1948.
Richardson, Alan. *A Preface to Bible Study.* Philadelphia: West-
minster Press, 1944.
Rowley, H. H. *The Relevance of the Bible.* New York: The
Macmillan Co., 1944.
Swaim, J. Carter. *Right and Wrong Ways to Use the Bible.*
Philadelphia: Westminster Press, 1953.
Watts, Harold H. *The Modern Reader's Guide to the Bible.*
New York: Harper & Bros., 1949.

III. On the Old Testament:

Bewer, Julius A. *The Literature of the Old Testament.* New
York: Columbia University Press, 1922, 1933.
Goodspeed, Edgar J. *The Story of the Old Testament.* Chicago:
University of Chicago Press, 1934.
James, Fleming. *Personalities of the Old Testament.* New York:
Charles Scribner's Sons, 1939.
Knopf, Carl S. *The Old Testament Speaks.* New York: Ronald
Press Co., 1933.

IV. On the New Testament:

Barnett, Albert. *The New Testament: Its Making and Meaning.*
New York: Abingdon-Cokesbury Press, 1946.
Craig, Clarence T. *The Beginning of Christianity.* New York:
Abingdon-Cokesbury Press, 1943.
Dodd, C. H. *About the Gospels.* New York: Cambridge Univer-
sity Press, 1950.
Goodspeed, Edgar J. *The Story of the New Testament.* Chicago:
University of Chicago Press, 1916.
Heard, Richard G. *An Introduction to the New Testament.* New
York: Harper & Bros., 1950.
Lyman, Mary Ely. *The Christian Epic.* New York: Charles
Scribner's Sons, 1936.
Scott, Ernest F. *The Literature of the New Testament.* New
York: Columbia University Press, 1932.

INDEX

Aaron, 62, 118
Abraham, 37, 42, 45, 49, 60, 63, 102, 118
Acts, Book of, 16, 82, 86, 91, 96, 98, 132
Adam and Eve, 25 f., 60 f., 124
Agricultural society, 16, 43 f.
Alexander the Great, 14, 47
Amos, 15, 67 f., 81, 115 f.
Anthropomorphism, 61, 110
Antioch, 40 f., 87, 97
Antiochus Epiphanes, 17, 80
Apocalyptic literature, 16, 80, 82 f., 102–04, 126; second coming, 85, 88
Arabian desert, 32, 36 f.
Ashtoreth, 44
Asia Minor, 41, 86 ff., 104
Assyria, 17, 33, 36 ff., 46, 62, 68 f., 117
Athens, 41, 87
Atonement, 51, 130 f. See Cross; Redemption

Baal, 34, 44
Babylon, 36 ff., 44, 46 f., 103
Bethel, 50, 67
Bethlehem, 33, 83, 119

Caesarea, 34, 91
Caesarea Philippi, 85, 97
Canaan, 16, 32, 43 f., 60
Chosen people, 17, 73, 111, 118, 121
Chronicles, I and II, 59, 65
Church, founding of, 40, 81 f., 83, 86, 94, 98, 106, 120, 131
Circumcision, 63, 88

Colossians, 91 f.
Corinth, 41, 87 f., 89 f.
Corinthians, I and II, 25, 28, 89 f., 93, 125, 127
Court records, 57–59
Covenant, 17 f., 49, 51, 83, 111, 117 f.; new covenant, 71, 121
Creation, 14, 22, 63 ff., 112–14, 122, 124 f., 130
Cross, 84, 128, 130 f. See death of Jesus
Culture, the Bible in our, 9–13, 18; social setting of the Bible, 36, 42–49

Daniel, 17, 80, 83, 103
David, 17, 20, 35, 48, 50, 57 ff., 61, 65 f., 75, 79, 83; Jesus as son of David, 86, 119 f.
Dead Sea, 33 f., 40
Dead Sea Scrolls, 54
Democracy, biblical roots, 12, 121
Deuteronomy, "D" writings, 63
Diaspora (dispersion), 36, 44, 47
Dirge, 15, 76
Domitian, 101, 103

"E" narratives, 61 f., 65
Ecclesiastes, 15, 28, 78
Editors, 54, 60–64
Egypt, 17, 34, 36, 38–40, 42 f., 47, 60, 68, 118
Elijah, 11, 34, 66 f.
Elisha, 66 f.
Ephesians, 54, 87, 91 f.
Ephesus, 41, 89 f., 92, 100, 103
Esther, 15, 79
Eternal life, 126 f.

INDEX

INDEX

Rome, 17, 41, 86, 90 f., 92, 96, 103 f., 117
Ruth, 15, 79

Sadducees, 48, 126
Samaria, Samaritans, 33 ff., 38, 46, 48, 62
Samson, 11, 34, 61
Samuel, 20, 57, 62, 66
Samuel, I and II, 58 ff.
Saul, 11, 20, 34 f., 50, 57, 59
Science, the Bible and, 19, 22, 56, 113
Second Isaiah, 46, 72–74, 79, 112
Sermon on the Mount, 95, 97
Short stories, 15, 19, 78 f.
Sinai, Mt., 43, 118; Peninsula, 34, 38–40
Social setting of the Bible, 42–49
Solomon, 17, 19, 58, 120
Song of Solomon, 15, 76
Southern Kingdom, 17, 35, 46, 59 f.
Stephen, 99, 101
Storytellers, 60–64, 82

Synoptic Gospels, 96–101
Syria, 40, 97

Temple, 19 f., 46 f., 51, 62 f., 75, 84, 99
Ten Commandments, 27, 43, 64
Theme of the Bible, 14, 29, 56, 109
Thessalonians, I and II, 87 f.
Thessalonica, 41, 87
Timothy, I and II, 87, 106
Titus, 87, 90, 106
Triumphal entry, 84, 86, 116
Tyre, 34, 38

Ur, 37, 42
Urim and Thummim, 50

Wisdom literature, 15, 76–78
Word of God, the Bible as, 19–29. See Inspiration, Revelation

Zechariah, 74
Zephaniah, 74